THE FLORIDA DOMICILE HANDBOOK

THE FLORIDA DOMICILE HANDBOOK:
VITAL INFORMATION FOR NEW FLORIDA RESIDENTS

4th Edition

E. Michael Kilbourn and Brad A. Galbraith

with Joshua D. Rudnick

Brendan Kelly Publishing Inc.
2122 Highview Drive
Burlington, Ontario L7P 0P3
Canada
www.brendankellypublishing.com

ISBN 978-1-895997-46-0

Printed in the U.S.A.

Select image or cartoon licenses obtained through BigStockPhoto and CartoonStock.

To our clients who have allowed us to guide
them in their transition to a new life in the
Sunshine State and for trusting us
to partner with them in finding solutions
to their financial and estate planning goals.

– Mike and Brad

ACKNOWLEDGMENTS

No book worthy of reading is written without help. ***The Florida Domicile Handbook: Vital Information for New Florida Residents, 4th Edition,*** is no exception. Brad Galbraith and I are fortunate to have two excellent assistants, Carina Arias and Joan Gardner, respectively. They deserve credit for their help in transcribing, editing, verifying and helping us with our organization of the material. We are thankful for attorney David Ruben's assistance in researching the multitude of state laws that are referenced in this book and at www.wwmrglaw.com/domicile-information. Mollie Page, my friend, publicist and marketing consultant, is an extraordinary editor. Without her, this and prior versions of this book could not have been written. We are also thankful to Brendan Kelly, our publisher, for going beyond the norm to make the prior and current editions more fun and easier to read. We cannot thank Carina, Joan, David, Mollie and Brendan enough for their help in making ***The Florida Domicile Handbook, 4th Edition,*** a book that our readers will appreciate and enjoy!

The State of Florida, and its myflorida.com website, is a trove of great information that inspired and validated much of the information in this book.

We also want to thank Joshua D. Rudnick, Esq., a partner at Woods, Weidenmiller, Michetti, Rudnick & Galbraith, PLLC, who helped make Chapter 10 on how to purchase a home in Florida more comprehensive. His insights and keen legal acumen as an experienced Florida real estate attorney have helped thousands of new residents during the home buying or selling process.

CONTENTS

PREFACE

YOUR PASSPORT TO PARADISE

Congratulations! You are about to embark on a journey that will bring you closer to becoming a Floridian. Florida is a paradise waiting to be explored. And, like a passport, this helpful guide gives you access to a new world. Few states can claim as much history and diversity as Florida. Keep this book close because it has everything you need to appreciate the great Sunshine State's many benefits. From where to go to catch pompano to what tax breaks the state can offer your business, Florida is more than just your new home, it's your paradise found.

Are you ready to begin the journey to Florida Domicile? Keep this book handy and don't declare without it!

A record breaking 98 million people visited Florida in 2016, with approximately 1,000 people a day never leaving and eventually making it their domicile. And while each new resident has a story behind his or her migration to the state, all can attest to its tax-friendly climate. From retirees to businesses, it pays to move to Florida because the state government is kind to its residents.

With an average high temperature of 80°F and an average low temperature of a comfortable 65°F, Florida residents can expect to enjoy every day of the year. And don't worry if the weatherman predicts a little rain because most of the state is less than 180 miles wide and weather moves through fast due to several currents and the Gulf Stream. The National Oceanic and Atmospheric Administration predicts 115 days of rain each year. Once you become a Floridian, you'll soon realize that most rainstorms are seasonal, last 15-30 minutes and arrive in the late afternoon, giving you just enough time to relax and rehydrate indoors before venturing outdoors again.

One advantage of Florida is that it provides almost endless recreational opportunities. The state is nearly surrounded by water and has thousands of lakes and dozens of rivers. If you are a real water lover and always dreamed of having a boat behind your house, check out Chapter 10, Purchasing a Home in Florida.

The Sunshine State also provides its residents access to millions of acres of hunting land, countless indoor and outdoor shooting ranges and a robust hunting season. Chapter 13 will give you an overview of the state's gun laws and some of the many activities that are available.

Florida residents enjoy an idyllic life, sculpted by a variety of diverse lifestyle activities and cultural opportunities. Many celebrities and industry icons call the state home, making it a top hotspot destination for world travelers and trendsetters. Whether you enjoy peaceful walks through state parks, world-class shopping destinations, unique cultural arts centers, world-famous theme parks or unparalleled golf courses, Florida can deliver.

Apart from the lifestyle activities and cultural opportunities that Florida offers its residents, those who claim domicile will also enjoy considerable financial benefits, including:

- No state income tax
- Helpful asset protection laws
- No state estate or gift taxes
- No intangibles tax
- A favorable homestead exemption
- An annual cap on tax increases on your homestead valuation
- Portability of your savings on valuation when you relocate in Florida
- Estate planning advantages
- A friendly, pro-business environment

In the next 250+ pages, you will learn more about these benefits as well as many other financial incentives enjoyed by Florida residents. ***The Florida Domicile Handbook*** is an easy and fun read with step-by-step instructions and suggestions to help you establish domicile at your own pace. We've also included the most asked questions and our answers to a myriad of topics you may encounter during your journey. As an extra benefit to readers, new questions and topics are addressed regularly on Mike Kilbourn's blog, which you can find at www.kilbournassociates.com. Plus, co-author Brad Galbraith and his estate-planning team at Woods, Weidenmiller, Michetti, Rudnick & Galbraith, PLLC, have built an easy online request system that provides users with links to government website pages that outline any state-specific domicile or change-of-residency requirements. Find it at www.wwmrglaw.com/domicile-information.

Finally, to expedite your journey, we've compiled hundreds of interesting facts and useful data about Florida to help you gain a better understanding of the state's history, government, geography, attractions, natives, trivia, amenities and cultural heritage. You don't have to read it cover to cover in order to enjoy all the benefits of Florida or Florida domicile. In fact, it would be impossible to include all of them in just one book.

We recommend using this handbook as a guide during your evaluation of the benefits of Florida domicile. Pick and choose what fits your circumstances. Use it to inspire conversations with friends and family about your new life in Florida.

If you are compelled to learn more while visiting Florida, attend one of our free Florida domicile seminars. A calendar of upcoming seminar dates can be found at www.kilbournassociates.com. Furthermore, you can engage with us on Mike's blog (www.kilbournassociates.com) or follow him on Twitter (@mikekilbourn). Our goal is to arm new residents with the truth about domicile. If you have a question about any domicile-related information in this book, feel free to contact the authors. Bios and contact details are at the back of the book.

INTRODUCTION

A BRIEF HISTORY OF FLORIDA

Archaeological records indicate activity by human inhabitants in Florida about 14,000 years ago. European explorers in the 16th century collected the first written evidence of Florida natives. Florida was home to dozens of Native American tribes including the Timucua, Apalachee, Tekesta and Calusa. French explorer Jean Ribault described the Timucua as “gentile, courteous and of good nature.” Unfortunately, by the 17th century the majority of these natives (100,000) were decimated by exposure to diseases brought by the European settlers.

The pursuit of Florida colonization began in 1513 with Juan Ponce de León. During one attempt by Europeans, a significant historical event took place in a little town called Fort Mose between the years 1738 and 1740: Fort Mose became the site of the first legally sanctioned free black community in the United States.

For numerous decades, attempts at colonization by the Spaniards and French continued. Spain finally relinquished control and Florida became a U.S. Territory in 1821. Tallahassee became the new capital and General Andrew Jackson served as military governor until Congress ratified a territorial constitution. William P. Duval was voted Florida’s first civil governor and called the first Legislative Council into session in Pensacola on June 19, 1823.

A Map of Florida in 1870

Reprinted with permission of www.Bigstock.com

As a protected American territory, Florida migration intensified and many new residents established large working plantations. As they continued to move into Florida, the demand for land started to increase and this upset the Native American tribes. When the Seminole leader Osceola refused to give up his tribe's land, the Second Seminole War began. Sadly, in the end, Osceola and his people lost their fight. While some left voluntarily, others escaped south to the Everglades where many of their descendants remain.

In 1845, Florida became the 27th state to join the United States of America. During the presidential election of 1860, there were no Florida votes for Abraham Lincoln. Consequently, shortly after Lincoln's election, Florida became a part of the Confederate States of America.

Florida played a significant role during the American Civil War as it supplied the Confederacy with food, men and cotton. Interestingly, Tallahassee was the only Confederate state capital east of the Mississippi River not captured by Union forces during the war. Civil War history buffs can visit Olustee Battlefield State Historic Site, located just outside Lake City, which commemorates the largest battle fought in Florida during the American Civil War.

Even though the Confederacy was defeated in 1865, Florida's economy continued to grow as it continued to export lumber and developed a large-scale cattle industry. By the late 1800s, Florida development was on the rise and new railroads helped travelers relocate to or visit such cities as Tampa, West Palm Beach and Winter Park.

In the 1920s, land sales skyrocketed due to a burst of financial growth and mobility of the middle class. Not even the Great Depression and several severe hurricanes could hurt Florida's land boom frenzy. Investors purchased land by mail and newspapers across the country and coined Florida real estate as the new gold rush. The popularity of Florida flourished again in the 1930s with the construction of its first theme park, Cypress Gardens, in central Florida.

By the 1950s, Florida's land boom—spurred by GIs returning from World War II and new road and highway construction—was in full force. In the late 1960s, Walt Disney brought his California dream to Florida and began building Walt Disney World near Orlando, Florida. Its first park, Magic Kingdom, opened in 1971, followed by EPCOT (Experimental Prototype Community of Tomorrow) in 1982, Disney Hollywood Studios (formerly Disney-MGM Studios) in 1989 and Disney Animal Kingdom in 1998. At present, the theme park industry continues to expand and tourism to these destinations represents one of the most significant financial industries in Florida.

The Great Recession of 2008, provoked in part by a global financial market imbalance, an impending subprime mortgage crisis, high unemployment, trade imbalances and high levels of consumer debt, hurt the Florida real estate market severely. Many businesses were forced into bankruptcy and thousands of families lost their homes to foreclosure. In December 2013, economists predicted Florida would lead the emergence from the recession. Historically, Florida's population has grown at an annual rate of 2 percent. Signs of recovery began to emerge across the state as a March 2014 study by the University of Florida indicated that consumer confidence rose to 81, the highest since before the recession began in December 2007.

Low taxes and a warm climate are two undeniable reasons why people move to Florida's subtropical paradise. It's certainly no surprise that many major U.S. corporations have decided to expand operations or relocate headquarters to Florida; they want to take advantage of the agreeable tax climate along with the eager, capable workforce.

"We got to thinking – Florida has fish too and it's a lot warmer."

PART 1

BENEFITS OF FLORIDA DOMICILE

This is a very exciting time for you. Rejoice in your new Florida life and get ready to reap the benefits as you embark on a journey to join the growing ranks of transplants who took the right steps to "prove intent" and are now enjoying the advantages of paradise and Florida domicile.

Did you know that approximately 70 percent of Florida's population was born elsewhere? Studies show that most newcomers emigrate from our nation's eastern and mid-western states. But we also know that nearly 23 percent of this population was born outside the country. In fact, the cultural diversity of Florida is 7 percent higher than the national average.

Inarguably, the top three reasons people move to Florida are weather, low taxes and recreation. But, throughout this book, you will find many other great incentives for making Florida your permanent home. For one, the living costs in Florida are significantly less than in other warm destinations, which may explain why more than three times as many retirees choose Florida over California.

Another incentive is that Florida residents live longer than the typical American and, according to a 2016 study conducted by 24/7 Wall Street, certain places in Florida, such as the Naples-Immokalee-Marco Island metro area, have the longest life spans in the country, where life expectancy at birth is 83.5 years – 4.7 years longer than the expected lifespan of the typical American!

KEY DEER

Florida is home to the world's smallest white-tailed deer, the Key deer. Found only in the Florida Keys, they stand less than 3 feet at the shoulder and weigh from 60 to 80 pounds.

The Key deer population was extensively harmed by over-hunting before being placed on the banned list in the 1950s. The population has since been able to rise but still faces threats. Florida Fish and Wildlife Conservation Commission would like to remind all residents and visitors to the Florida Keys that feeding Key deer is not only dangerous for the animals it is also illegal. Feeding any wild animals can cause harm to them, as continuous feeding can result in dependence on people for food.

The Key Deer Wildlife Refuge on Big Pine Key is an ideal place to view this tiny endangered species.

Source: myfwc.com.

Those Beautiful Trees

Florida is home to hundreds of different species of trees but the palm tree is what most people associate with Florida. The royal palm can be recognized by its straight, silver-white trunk. Other palms found in Florida include the sabal palm, also known as the cabbage palm, and the coconut palm, which resembles the royal palm, but is thinner and adorned at the top with the distinctive coconut.

Another favorite tree, the gumbo limbo, takes its nickname, "the tourist tree," from its unique bark. Like visitors who have spent a long day at the beach, this tree's "skin" is also red and peeling.

Florida is home to cypress trees that grow in wet places along rivers, streams and creeks, as well as in swamps with slow moving water. A cypress can live up to 600 years. It is typically draped with Spanish moss and conspicuous for its cypress "knees"—buttresses from the tree that stick out of the water.

Live oaks can be found throughout the state. It is a familiar tree of massive size and density, weighing 55 pounds per cubic foot. Its acorns are a food source to many animals.

Reprinted with permission of Bigstock.com

Up and down Florida's southern coastline you can find mangroves. These trees are remarkable in their ability to survive in salt water by a process of natural desalination. The three main species of mangrove—the red mangrove, the white mangrove and the black mangrove—are hosts to many small marine animals and birds and are protected by many laws and regulations.

THE BANK JUST APPROVED OUR HOME EQUITY LOAN.
GREAT, NOW WE CAN PAY OUR PROPERTY TAXES!

The trouble with retirement is that you never get a day off.
–Abe Lemons

CHAPTER 1

THE FLORIDA ADVANTAGE

Tax Advantages

Florida is one of only seven states that does **not** impose an income tax on its residents. After Florida eliminated its intangible personal property tax in 2007, it has consistently ranked as one of the most tax-friendly states in the country. In fact, in terms of having a favorable tax climate, Florida ranks first in the nation for individual income taxes and fourth overall as the best state in which to live and do business, according to the Tax Foundation's 2017 State Business Tax Climate Index.

A provision in the Economic Growth and Tax Relief Reconciliation Act (EGTRRA) of 2001 eliminated the sharing of federal estate tax revenues with the states. Consequently, many states adopted a separate form of estate tax but Florida did not. And, no matter what happens on the federal level, Florida is constitutionally bound to allow its citizens to decide their fate regarding a state estate tax through the constitutional amendment process. As a result, it seems unlikely that Florida will ever have a separate estate tax. You will discover more Florida tax benefits in Chapter 2.

Asset Protection Advantages

When you declare domicile in Florida, certain assets are protected from the claims of your creditors like your homestead, retirement plans, life insurance, annuities, assets held in a properly structured limited liability company, certain types of partnerships and, in many cases, wage accounts. This protection is generally unlimited; however, many advantages of asset protection are not available, or are limited, when personal bankruptcy is involved.

For instance, retirement plans—including individual retirement accounts (IRAs) and Roth IRA accounts—normally enjoy protection from attachment by creditors in Florida. Even so, keep in mind, when personal bankruptcy is involved, the amount exempted under the 2005 Bankruptcy Law is limited to one million dollars unless the owner can demonstrate that the excess amount represents rollover distributions from one or more qualified retirement plans.

Additional asset protection strategies, especially relating to estate planning for Florida residents, are discussed in Chapter 4.

The Real Estate Market

Real estate values indicate that Florida is one of the most desirable locations in the world. According to Florida Realtors®, there are approximately 155,000 registered REALTORS® in the state vying to sell thousands of homes where the median sale price in April 2017 was around $234,900.

President Donald Trump bought a seven-acre oceanfront estate in Palm Beach for $41 million in 2004 and later sold it for $95 million. Even if your budget isn't on par with Trump's, it is not impossible to find your dream home in a beautiful Florida paradise.

Economists at Florida Realtors® contend Florida homeowners and homebuyers continue to benefit from low mortgage rates, high home affordability, strong home price growth, increasing home values and a steadily improving job market. With the buying tips we provide in Chapter 10, you will discover how to search, negotiate and borrow, so that you can own a piece of paradise.

Property Tax Advantages

The mechanism for assessing real estate property taxes provides another Florida tax advantage. Residents can limit their exposure to increased real estate taxes on their homes through the homestead exemption and the associated limitation on tax assessments known as the Save Our Homes (SOH) Amendment to the Florida Constitution, which we cover in Chapter 3.

After you purchase a home and declare Florida domicile, you may qualify for a homestead tax exemption of $50,000 by simply applying for the exemption. The first $25,000 applies to all property taxes, including school district taxes. The additional exemption, up to $25,000, applies to the assessed value between $50,000 and $75,000 and only to non-school taxes. Depending upon the Florida county where you establish your domicile, the combination of the two exemptions will generally save approximately $400 to $800 in property taxes per year. Low-income seniors and certain disabled veterans can receive additional Florida homestead benefits. Learn more about the advantages of Florida's homestead exemption laws, including the Save Our Homes Amendment, in Chapter 3.

Estate Planning Advantages

Floridians are fortunate to have a significant number of top financial advisors and estate-planning professionals who can assist in managing and planning your estate. In order to properly protect yourself and your family, you must understand estate planning and the options available to you. Issues to consider include probate avoidance, federal estate tax minimization, planning for disability from a financial and health care perspective, eventual distribution options, protections available to beneficiaries and how to keep your plan up-to-date. We discuss these topics in Chapter 4.

Interesting Florida Facts

Nickname: "The Sunshine State"
State motto: "In God We Trust"
State anthem: "Florida (where the Sawgrass Meets the Sky)" by Jan Hinton
State song: "The Swanee River (Old Folks At Home)" by Stephen C. Foster
State tree: Sabal Palm
State flower: Orange Blossom
State animal: Florida Panther
State bird: Mockingbird
State reptile: American Alligator
State marine mammal: West Indian Manatee
State freshwater fish: Largemouth Bass
State saltwater fish: Sailfish
State shell: Horse Conch
State fruit: Orange
State beverage: Orange Juice
State pie: Key Lime Pie
Number of people who move to Florida each day: 1,000
Miles of sand beaches: 825
Miles of coastline: 1,197
Number of golf courses: 1,000+
County with the most golf courses: Palm Beach County
Number of hotel rooms in Florida: 370,000+
Number of state parks in Florida: 171
Number of islands: 4,500

Sources: *MyFlorida.com, flheritage.com/facts/symbols, flheritage.com/facts/quickfacts, Florida State Parks*

Career Opportunities

With so many people choosing to make Florida their home and so many businesses relocating to the Sunshine State, there are constantly increasing options for those seeking employment and career opportunities. Chapter 5 discusses the many benefits of locating your business in Florida. Also, Appendix A lists several websites that focus on helping you find job opportunities.

Weather

Florida's climate is one of its best attributes. In fact, the state's enviable climate gives rise to its nickname: The Sunshine State. The moderate to warm winter temperatures, cool sea breezes and tropical summers make Florida a premier choice for living, learning, working and playing. It is no secret that the over 112 million annual visitors—generating billions of dollars in economic activity—flock to Florida because of the great weather.

On average, winter weather remains mild to warm throughout Florida. Lows range from 41°F (5°C) in Tallahassee to 65°F (18°C) in Key West while daytime highs vary from 64°F (18°C) in Tallahassee to 77°F (25°C) in Miami. Predominant easterly winds across southern Florida keep temperatures moderate during the winter, as the nearby Gulf Stream warms cooler air moving in from the northeast and east.

During the summer, lows range from near 70°F (21°C) in northern Florida to near 80°F (27°C) in the Florida Keys and high temperatures average in the upper 80s and low 90s Fahrenheit statewide. Relief from the heat during the summer comes in the form of afternoon and evening thunderstorm activity with late morning and afternoon sea breezes off the relatively cooler Atlantic Ocean and Gulf of Mexico.

Recreation

Florida boasts a nearly endless list of outdoor recreational activities and includes exceptional fishing, golfing at one of the more than 1,358 public and private golf courses, hiking and picnicking at any of the 171 state parks and 9 state trails, sunning and swimming along the 825 miles of sandy beaches, touring the many theme parks, including Walt Disney World, SeaWorld and Universal Orlando Resort, and visiting one of the many world class resorts including several Ritz-Carlton resorts. The list goes on but you get the idea.

Cultural Events

While enjoying the wonderful weather in Florida, you can choose from literally thousands of cultural events, such as the Tampa Bay Caribbean Carnival, the Nine Mile Music Festival in Miami, the Chasco Fiesta™ in New Port Richie, the Hollywood Beach Latin Festival, Fantasy Fest in Key West or Summer Jazz on the Gulf in Naples.

Even More Advantages

Moving to Florida now and declaring it as your domicile comes with countless advantages that positively affect every aspect of life—not to mention allowing you to spend carefree days enjoying its golden sunshine and limitless recreational options.

In order to provide you with comprehensive information that will make changing your domicile to Florida easier, we have included chapters on Changing Your Domicile—a Step-by-Step Guide (Chapter 6), Florida Driver Licenses and Motor Vehicles (Chapter 7), Registering to Vote in Florida (Chapter 8), Purchasing a Home in Florida (Chapter 10), Florida Insurance and Health Care Options (Chapter 11) and Florida Education Options (Chapter 12). In the following pages, we hope you will discover a wealth of Florida facts and trivia to inspire you to live your Florida life to its fullest.

5 Common Florida Myths

1.) I'll be attacked by a shark if I go swimming at the beach.
You are 75 times more likely to be struck by lightning than be attacked by a shark in Florida. In fact, shark attacks are down in Florida, due to increased education and awareness.

2.) A hurricane will destroy my Florida home.
Since 1851, only two Category 5 and eight Category 4 hurricanes have hit Florida. Mandatory building codes require new structures be built to withstand hurricane force winds. Therefore, it is unlikely that your home will be destroyed.

3.) I will get skin cancer if I move to Florida.
Skin cancer is one of the most preventable cancers. Interestingly, most dermatologists will tell you that the majority of sun damage (and its potential problems) is obtained before you reach adulthood. Apply sunblock whenever you go outdoors (even on overcast days). Also, avoid direct sunlight between 10 a.m. and 2 p.m. when the sun's rays are strongest.

4.) An alligator is going to bite my leg off.
Officials with the Florida Fish and Wildlife Conservation Commission say alligators seldom bite people and fatalities from such occurrences are extremely rare. If an alligator happens to venture into a body of water near your residence and poses a threat to people, pets or property, call (866) FWC-GATOR.

5.) I won't be able to earn a living wage in Florida.
Florida's economy grew 3 percent in 2016, outpacing the nation's 1.5 percent. Florida also holds nine spots on a recent list by Forbes of the "Top 25 Fastest-Growing Cities in 2017." New transplants, many of whom are retired, will put a demand on Florida businesses and the workforce will grow.

Sources: *Florida Museum of Natural History, U.S. Bureau of Economic Analysis*

"What the ... They raised our property tax assessment 21 percent because we added a birdbath!"

The taxpayer: that's someone who works for the federal government but doesn't have to take a civil service examination.
–Ronald Reagan

CHAPTER 2

FLORIDA TAXES

Even with a 2018 state budget of $82.4 billion, one of the most attractive financial reasons to choose Florida as your domicile is the relatively low tax rate. Depending on the state you are moving from, you could experience significant tax relief.

Florida provides an ideal tax climate for both retirees and businesses. The state ranks low in terms of the tax burden placed on residents. Based on data from the U.S. Census Bureau and the Internal Revenue Service, the Tax Foundation—a nonpartisan educational organization that helps consumers understand tax policy—and others, Florida ranks fourth among the states with the lowest overall state tax burden. Estimated at 6.79 percent of income, Florida's state and local tax burden (comparing such things as state and local income tax, real estate tax, vehicle tax, sales and use tax, fuel tax, alcohol tax, telecom tax and food tax) ranks 45th nationally.

No State Income Tax

Florida is one of only seven states, including Alaska, Nevada, South Dakota, Texas, Washington and Wyoming, without a *personal income tax*. This benefit alone could constitute reason enough to make Florida your permanent domicile and may represent substantial savings to you, your family and your employees. No state income tax means the revenue you generate from employment and your investment earnings is free to grow without the burden of a high state-imposed tax rate. For example, if your domicile is currently Minnesota, depending upon your level of income, the state income tax ranges from 5.35 to 9.85 percent of your income (including Social Security) each year.

Interestingly, the Florida Constitution specifically prohibits imposing a state income tax. It is unlikely that Florida voters will ever vote to add a state income tax.

To illustrate the benefit of zero state income tax in Florida, let's assume that in 2017 a married couple earned $70,000 each in wages plus an additional $10,000 in combined interest and dividend income for a total adjusted gross income (AGI) of $150,000. Suppose also that they had no itemized deductions. The state income tax for Florida is zero. However, in many other states the picture, as shown below, is quite different:

Michigan tax = $6,035 (flat tax of 4.25 percent after personal exemptions of $8,000)

California tax = $15,450 (graduated tax to a high of 13.3 percent)

Pennsylvania tax = $4,605 (flat tax at 3.07 percent)

Even though Florida does not have an income tax, if that same couple is domiciled in Florida and receives a salary from rental income in real estate or a business entity located in a different state, that state would continue to have the right to impose its own income tax on that income.

No Estate, Inheritance or Gift Tax

The federal government no longer shares *estate tax* revenues with individual states (see chart on next page). In response, many

STATE	INHERITANCE TAX?	ESTATE TAX?
Alabama	No	No
Alaska	No	No
Arizona	No	No
Arkansas	No	No
California	No	No
Colorado	No	No
Connecticut	No	**Yes**
Delaware	No	No
District of Columbia	No	**Yes**
FLORIDA	NO	NO
Georgia	No	No
Hawaii	No	**Yes**
Idaho	No	No
Illinois	No	**Yes**
Indiana	No	No
Iowa	**Yes**	No
Kansas	No	No
Kentucky	**Yes**	No
Louisiana	No	No
Maine	No	**Yes**
Maryland	**Yes**	**Yes**
Massachusetts	No	**Yes**
Michigan	No	No
Minnesota	No	**Yes**
Mississippi	No	No
Missouri	No	No
Montana	No	No
Nebraska	**Yes**	No
Nevada	No	No
New Hampshire	No	No
New Jersey	**Yes**	No
New Mexico	No	No
New York	No	**Yes**
North Carolina	No	No
North Dakota	No	No
Ohio	No	No
Oklahoma	No	No
Oregon	No	**Yes**
Pennsylvania	**Yes**	No
Rhode Island	No	**Yes**
South Carolina	No	No
South Dakota	No	No
Tennessee	No	No
Texas	No	No
Utah	No	No
Vermont	No	**Yes**
Virginia	No	No
Washington	No	**Yes**
West Virginia	No	No
Wisconsin	No	No
Wyoming	No	No

states have "decoupled" from the federal estate tax system, meaning that those states have established their own gift, estate and/or inheritance taxes.

Florida is one of only three states whose state constitution requires voter approval for the imposition of a state *inheritance or gift tax.* Consequently, Florida has no current estate or gift taxes and is unlikely to have any in the future—without a change in the Florida Constitution by Florida voters. This could provide substantial savings for your heirs.

For example, in 2017, if you were domiciled in and passed away in Maryland, which decoupled from the federal system, your estate would be exposed to a state estate tax of 16 percent above a $3 million exemption plus a 10 percent inheritance tax on every dollar left to a niece, nephew, friend or partner. Under current law, for deaths in 2018, an estate with a gross value of more than $4 million may owe the Maryland estate tax and, in 2019, this exemption amount will match the federal estate tax exemption. The tax due is in addition to any federal estate tax due.

Note that even though Florida does not impose its own estate or gift tax, if you own real estate or other tangible assets in another state, your heirs may be subject to an estate and/or inheritance tax in that state—based on the value of those specific assets. With proper planning and depending upon state law, it may be possible to avoid these state estate taxes if those out-of-state assets are held in a separate entity such as a Family Limited Liability Company (see Chapter 4 for more details).

State laws change frequently but, as of 2018, 16 states—Connecticut, Hawaii, Illinois, Iowa, Kentucky, Maine, Maryland, Massachusetts, Minnesota, New Jersey, New York, Oregon, Pennsylvania, Rhode Island, Vermont, Washington and the District of Columbia—either decoupled from the federal changes (the sharing arrangement that ended) to establish their own separate state estate tax and/or have established a separate state inheritance tax. Estate taxes are based on the value of the estate as a whole, whereas inheritance taxes are based on who actually inherits the estate. As seen in the chart on the page 15, six states collect an inheritance tax. They are: Iowa, Kentucky, Maryland, Nebraska, New Jersey and Pennsylvania. One state, Maryland, imposes both a state estate tax and an inheritance tax.

No Intangibles Tax

An *intangibles tax* is a state tax on intangible assets, such as stocks, bonds, notes, etc. In 2006, the Florida legislature and the governor repealed the state's long-standing Florida intangibles tax, effective January 1, 2007. Therefore, newcomers need not worry about filing a Florida intangibles tax form or paying any tax on intangible assets. This makes Florida one of the very few states that do not charge either an income tax or intangibles tax and, thus, Florida can truly be called a tax haven.

Sales Tax

Florida law provides that each sale, admission charge, storage fee or rental is taxable, along with some services, unless the transaction is specifically exempt. The current *state sales tax* rate is 6 percent. This amounts to considerably less than the average state sales tax in the United States of 8.454 percent (excluding four states, Delaware, Montana, New Hampshire and Oregon, that have no sales tax).

Discretionary Sales Surtax

Under specific conditions, Florida counties are authorized to levy a *discretionary sales surtax* on most transactions that are subject to sales and use tax. The tax is determined by the county where the merchandise or service is delivered and ranges from 0.5 to 1.5 percent and is in addition to the six percent state sales tax.

Only the first $5,000 of a single sale of tangible personal property is subject to the discretionary sales surtax if the property is sold as a single item, in bulk, as a working unit or as part of a working unit. Items that are not normally sold as a set or unit cannot be combined to qualify for the $5,000 limit and are taxed at the normal discretionary sales surtax rate. Also, the $5,000 limit does not apply to commercial rentals, transient rentals or services.

For example, a $6,000 piano delivered to a home in a Florida county imposing a 1.0 percent discretionary sales surtax would have the following tax:

$6,000 × 6 percent (sales tax)	$360
$5,000 × 1 percent (surtax)	+$50
Total tax due	**$410**

If you reside in one of the 67 Florida counties that imposes a surtax—which can vary from time to time—and purchase an automobile, boat or aircraft to be titled in your name, the dealer is required to collect the surtax at the county rate. For example, if you lived in Miami-Dade County in 2017 and purchased a $35,000 automobile to be titled in your name, the following tax would apply:

$35,000 × 6 percent (sales tax)	$2,100
$5,000 × 1 percent (surtax)	+ $50
Total tax due	**$2,150**

A list of Florida counties, their discretionary sales surtax rates and appropriate dates are published each year on Form DR-15DSS. Rates and forms are available online at www.myflorida.com/dor. Contact information for the Florida Department of Revenue is included at the end of this chapter.

Use Tax

Use tax complements and is applied in the same manner as sales tax. Unless specifically exempt, use tax is due on purchases made out of state and brought into Florida within six months of the purchase

Discretionary Sales Surtax on Taxable Items (Local Option County Tax)				
If a vendor located in any Florida county	with a discretionary surtax	sells & delivers	into the county where the selling vendor is located,	surtax is collected at the county rate where the delivery is made.
If a vendor located in any Florida county	with or without a discretionary surtax	sells & delivers	into counties with different discretionary surtax rates,	surtax is collected at the county rate where the delivery is made.
If a vendor located in any Florida county	with or without a discretionary surtax	sells & delivers	into counties without a discretionary surtax,	surtax is not collected.
If an out-of-state vendor		sells & delivers	into a Florida county with a discretionary surtax,	surtax is collected at the county rate where the delivery is made.
If an out-of-state vendor		sells & delivers	into a Florida county without a discretionary surtax,	surtax is not collected.
Source: Florida Department of Revenue, dor.myflorida.com/dor/taxes/discretionary.html.				

date. The use tax rate and the sales tax rate are the same, including the additional discretionary sales surtax, if applicable.

Examples of taxable purchases include such things as an automobile purchased in another state, furniture delivered from a dealer located in another state, computer equipment purchased from an out-of-state computer firm and so forth.

Purchased items used in another state for six months or longer are not subject to the use tax when they are brought into Florida. Also, no tax is due if the out-of-state dealer charged sales tax of six percent or more. If the dealer charged less than six percent, you are required to pay the difference.

For example, if, as a Florida resident, you purchased an automobile and brought it into Florida within six months after the purchase and the dealer charged four percent sales tax, you must pay the additional two percent tax to Florida. This is similar to how most other states treat the purchase of tangible personal property from other states.

To file and pay the use tax, you must complete an out-of-state purchase return form (DR-15MO). You can retrieve this form from the website floridarevenue.com. For additional assistance, contact the Florida Department of Revenue using the phone numbers listed in the table at the end of this chapter.

Sales and Use Tax on Residential Rentals

Florida home owners who rent their home, condominium or other residential real estate (i.e., garage apartment, beach house, cottage, time share, mobile home, boats with a permanent fixed location, apartment-hotels, motels, rooming houses, etc.) in Florida to another person for a period of six (6) months *or less* must pay a six percent tax on the amount of rent received. The additional cost is frequently passed on to the tenant as an addition to the rent paid.

For example, if you collect monthly rent of $4,000 for a home that you are leasing for six months or less, the rent is taxed at the rate of six percent as follows:

Monthly tax = 6 percent × $4,000 = $240

Tourist Development Tax

Most counties have a discretionary sales surtax, local option tax, *tourist development tax*, convention development tax or tourist impact tax on rentals of "transient accommodations." This means they are rented for periods of six months or less. These include living quarters in hotels, apartment-hotels, motels, resort motels, rooming houses, trailer camps, cooperatively owned apartments, multiple-unit structures, mobile homes, trailers, single-family dwellings, beach houses, cottages and condominiums.

For example, in Collier County, Florida, there is a Tourist Development Tax of four percent on all rental income received from accommodations rented for six (6) months or less. Thus, if you owned a home in Collier County that you leased out for six months or less, you would owe sales tax of six percent plus a Tourist Development Tax of four percent on all rental income.

Sales and Use Tax on Commercial Real Property Rentals

Sales tax is due at the rate of 6 percent on the total rent paid or the right to use or occupy commercial real property (i.e., office or retail space, warehouses, convention and meeting rooms, mini-warehouse space, etc.), unless the rent is specifically exempt. If the tenant makes payments such as mortgage, *ad valorem* taxes or insurance on behalf of the landlord, those payments are also classified as rent and are subject to tax. Payments for separately stated services (i.e., common area maintenance or CAM) that are required under the lease or license are part of the taxable total rent paid.

Rental payments subject to sales tax are also subject to any locally imposed discretionary sales surtax. The surtax rate is determined by the rate imposed by the county in which the property is located. On a single sale of tangible personal property, only the first $5,000 is subject to discretionary sales surtax. However, this $5,000 limitation does not apply to taxable rentals of commercial real properties. On taxable rentals of commercial real properties, the entire rental payment is subject to discretionary sales surtax. Obtain additional information online at floridarevenue.com/Forms_library/current/dr15tdt.pdf.

Real Property (*Ad Valorem*) Tax

If you own a home or other real estate in Florida, the county appraiser will assess the value, as of January 1st each year, and the county tax collector, in the county where the property is located, will collect taxes on it.

Each county determines its own millage or tax rate (per $1,000 of valuation), according to that county's budget needs. The assessed value is multiplied by the tax rate to calculate the tax, which is billed in November and due by April 1st of the following year. If you build your homestead, the property appraiser will not assess its improved value until after the county issues a certificate of occupancy.

For example, if the Florida county where you own your homestead assesses the value at $500,000 and you subtract the Florida Homestead Exemption of $50,000, assuming the total millage rate for the current tax year is $11.5 per thousand dollars of valuation, the total current tax due would be calculated in two steps, as follows:

Shelling by the Seashore

Shelling is a pastime Floridians of all ages enjoy. Here are some tips that will help you get the best finds for your time.

- Make sure to check the local newspaper for tide charts. The best times to shell are immediately before and after low tide.
- Bad weather might ruin your day at the beach but a storm can bring to the shore some amazing finds.
- Winter is the optimal season for shelling. Thankfully for Floridians, a light sweater is all you will need during the hunt.
- The early bird gets the worm. Get to the beach early in the morning to have first pick at Neptune's treasures.
- While most shells that wash ashore have lost their host, a Florida recreational saltwater fishing license is required in order to harvest a sea shell containing a living organism, even from a public beach. Also, many counties have limits on the number of live shells that can be harvested.

Source: *Travel and Leisure, myfwc.com*

Homestead valuation reduction: \$500,000 - \$50,000 = \$450,000

Tax = 11.5 × (\$450,000/\$1,000) = \$5,175

Note: This example is a simplification, as \$25,000 of the \$50,000 Homestead Exemption does not apply to the school tax portion of an actual tax calculation. Thus, in order to properly calculate the school tax portion of the property tax bill, you should use the smaller Homestead Exemption of \$25,000.

Non-Homestead Properties

Due to the Florida Constitutional Save Our Homes (SOH) Amendment passed by voters on January 29, 2008, there is an assessment growth limitation of ten percent for all non-homestead properties, subject to the following limitations:

- The assessment limitation does not apply to school tax levies;
- The assessment limitation will expire ten years from enactment—at which time, voters will decide whether to reauthorize it;
- Residential properties of nine units or less will surrender accumulated protections (no portability) at change of ownership or control;
- For all other properties (i.e., residential properties of ten or more units and business properties), the Legislature must define how the property will surrender protections when there is a qualifying improvement to the property;
- The Legislature may define how the property will surrender accumulated protections at a change of ownership or control; and
- The cap uses 2008 as its base year.

A detailed discussion of the Homestead Exemption and how the SOH Amendment affects homestead properties is included in the next chapter.

Tangible Personal Property

The same Florida Constitutional SOH Amendment passed on January 29, 2008, created an exemption of $25,000 for tangible personal property for businesses. Thus, business owners with tangible personal property (i.e., computers, copiers, fax machines, etc.) worth less than $25,000 and used in their businesses do not have to file detailed returns and will owe no tax. This exemption applies to school tax levies as well.

Documentary Stamp Tax

Florida assesses a tax on promissory notes, mortgages, bonds, security agreements and other written promises to pay money. The basic tax is 35 cents per $100 with a limit of $2,450 on notes and other written obligations and no limit for the tax due for mortgages and liens filed and recorded in Florida. On all documents that convey an interest in real estate, however, the tax is 70 cents per $100 (the Miami-Dade County rate is 60 cents on all documents plus 45 cents per $100 surtax on documents transferring anything other than a single-family residence).

For example, on a $40,000 promissory note, the tax would be assessed at the rate of 35 cents per $100 of value and is calculated as follows:

Tax = $0.35 × ($40,000/$100) = $140

For large promissory loan amounts, the documentary stamp tax is capped at $2,450.

On the transfer of a parcel of Florida real estate valued at one million dollars, the tax is based on 70 cents per $100 of value and is calculated as follows:

Florida: A Golfer's Dream

With more golf courses than any other destination in the world, it is no wonder golfers choose Florida as the place to vacation and, ultimately, reside. From Pensacola to Key West and from Jacksonville to Naples, Florida has more than 1,000 courses to test the skill level of any player. And Florida's climate allows you to enjoy the sport 365 days a year.

If you just like to watch, Florida is home to the PGA Tour, Champions Tour, LPGA, PGA of America, World Golf Hall of Fame and several other professional golf tours. In fact, more professional golfers live in Florida than in any other state.

Founded in 1916, The PGA of America is the largest working sports organization in the world, comprised of more than 28,000 dedicated men and women promoting the game of golf to everyone, everywhere. Discover tournaments in Florida at www.pga.com.

The Club at Pelican Bay in Naples

photo courtesy of Teresa Kelly

Tax = $0.70 × ($1,000,000/$100) = $7,000

Florida Business Taxes

While a discussion of the possible taxes affecting a Florida business is beyond the scope of this book, there are five taxes with which every business owner should be familiar. They are:

- Sales and use tax,
- Discretionary sales surtax,
- Unemployment tax,
- Communications services tax and
- Corporate income tax.

More information about the tax advantages for Florida businesses is discussed in Chapter 5. Additionally, many local agencies, such as the Small Business Administration, can help new residents set up a business. And the Department of Revenue (DOR) service centers located within the state host educational seminars about Florida's taxes. This could prove especially helpful if you are starting a new business or planning to move your business to Florida.

Additional Resources

More detailed information on Florida's personal and business taxes is located in the DOR Tax Rules. Tax publications are available on the department's website: www.myflorida.com/dor/taxes.

Contact the Department of Revenue

General questions:	(800) 352-3671
Hearing/speech impaired:	TDD (800) 367-8331 or (850) 922-1115
DOR Distribution Center:	(850) 488-8422
Address for a written reply to tax questions:	Taxpayer Services Florida Department of Revenue 5050 West Tennessee Street Tallahassee, FL 32304-2716
Order copies online:	www.myflorida.com/dor/forms
Fax form requests to:	(850) 922-2208
Mail form requests to:	Distribution Center Florida Department of Revenue 168A Blountstown Highway Tallahassee, FL 32304-2702

Note: Taxpayer Services is open Monday through Friday, 8 a.m. to 7 p.m. ET.

An Endangered Predator

Reprinted with permission of Bigstock.com

The unique and beautiful Florida panther (Puma concolor coryi) has been on the Endangered Species List since 1973. This big, graceful tan-colored cat makes its home in South Florida, where it hunts deer and other game. Much of the state's research funding to study and protect the Florida panther is financed by sales of the Florida panther specialty license plate. The main threat facing the panther today is loss of habitat. Florida Fish and Wildlife estimates panther population is on the rise from an estimated 100-180 in 2014 to 120-230 in 2017.

Source: *Big Cat Rescue, Tampa, FL, myfwc.com*

PROPERTY
TAX
BILL

Real estate cannot be lost or stolen, nor can it be carried away. Purchased with common sense, paid for in full and managed with reasonable care, it is about the safest investment in the world.
–Franklin D. Roosevelt

CHAPTER 3

FLORIDA HOMESTEAD EXEMPTION

A Florida homestead has been called a "legal chameleon" because the notion of "homestead status" may change, depending upon the situation. Florida homestead laws have three aspects that are important to residents: 1.) the real estate tax exemption for homestead (commonly referred to as the homestead tax exemption) and its related component, known as the "Save Our Homes" Amendment to the Florida Constitution, 2.) protection from a forced sale of the homestead by a creditor (asset protection) and 3.) "devise and descent" issues for a surviving spouse and minor children. All these aspects have the same purpose: to protect the owner of the homestead and his/her heirs.

Homestead Tax Exemption

Every resident domiciled in Florida on January 1st is eligible to receive a homestead exemption of up to $50,000. The first $25,000 applies to all property taxes, including school district taxes. The additional exemption, up to $25,000, applies to the assessed value between $50,000 and $75,000 and only to non-school taxes.

The application for homestead exemption (Form DR-501) and other property tax forms can be found online at floridarevenue.

com/dor/property/forms/current/dr501.pdf and on most property appraiser's sites. Some county sites have quick and easy online applications. If filing for the first time, be prepared to answer these questions:

- Whose name or names were recorded on the title on January 1st?
- What is the street address of the property?
- Were you living in the dwelling on January 1st?
- Do you claim homestead in another county or state?

If one spouse holds the title, the other spouse may file for the exemption with the consent of the titleholder-spouse. To prove you have changed your domicile, the property appraiser may ask for any of the following:

- Previous residency outside Florida and date ended
- Florida driver license or alternative Florida ID card number
- Evidence of giving up driver license from other state
- Florida vehicle tag number
- Florida voter registration number (if US citizen)
- The date of your Declaration of Domicile
- Current employer
- Address listed on your last IRS return
- School location of dependent children
- Bank statement and checking account mailing address
- Proof of payment (i.e., paid bills) of utilities at homestead address

The courts in Florida have been very generous in allowing the homestead tax exemption to apply to all sorts of home ownership, not merely for the traditional single-family home but also for condominiums, cooperative apartments and certain types of mobile homes.

For Florida residents who qualify for and have received the homestead exemption, a significant additional tax benefit is available due to the Save Our Homes Amendment to the Florida Constitution.

Save Our Homes Amendment

The Save Our Homes (SOH) Amendment to the Florida Constitution is a special component of the Florida homestead exemption and could represent substantial savings over a period of years to you and your family. This Amendment, which became effective January 1, 1995, places a limitation or cap on the percentage increase in annual tax assessment of the value of a residence that qualifies for the homestead exemption. The cap is the lower of the increase in the consumer price index (CPI) or 3 percent of the assessed value of the home each year following the year you receive your homestead exemption.

There has been quite a bit of confusion concerning the workings of the Save Our Homes Amendment. A simple example will help. Assume you became a Florida resident on or before December 31, 2017; you then would have until March 1, 2018, to file for Florida's Homestead Exemption and that exemption would be effective January 1, 2018. The 3 percent valuation cap, however, would apply to the following year, 2019. Thus, if you established homestead in 2018 and received your exemption, even if the county property appraiser increased your assessed value to the then fair market value for 2018, the 3 percent valuation cap would not apply to your assessed valuation until 2019.

If you had postponed changing your domicile to Florida until January 1, 2018, and subsequently filed for homestead, you would not be able to secure the Homestead Exemption for the same year you changed your domicile to Florida (2018), even if you filed for homestead by March 1, 2018. In effect, you would be "filing early" for the following year—2019. In this case, you could wait and file for the Florida homestead exemption as late as March 1, 2019, to obtain the Homestead Exemption for 2019. The 3 percent cap would come into play the following year, which, in this example, would be 2020.

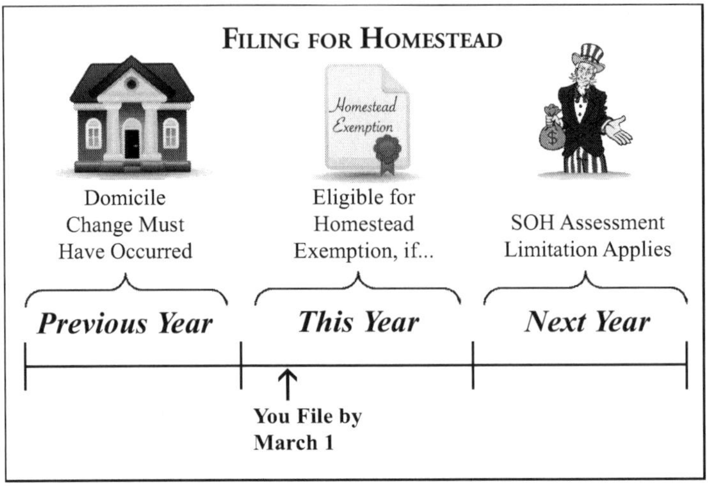

Portability

On January 29, 2008, Florida voters approved a change to the Florida Constitution that allows for the portability of accumulated SOH benefits for homeowners who move from one Florida homestead to another. The new law provides the following:

Homeowners may transfer their SOH benefit, up to $500,000, to a new Florida homestead within two years of leaving their former homestead. For example, if you sold your home and moved during 2018, the exemption remains on your home until December 31, 2018. You have until January 1, 2020, to qualify for a new exemption and "port" the benefit to a new homestead (technically, you have until March 1, 2020, in this example, to qualify for portability). The SOH benefit can be transferred to a newly acquired residence anywhere in the state of Florida and is calculated differently, depending on whether the purchase price of the new residence is greater (upsizing)

The Florida Blueprint

Total area: 58,560 square miles (land and water)
Land area: 54,136 square miles
Total water area: 4,424 square miles
Rank among states in total area: 22nd
Length north to south: 447 miles
Width east to west: 361 miles
Distance from Pensacola to Key West: 792 miles by road
Highest natural point: 345 feet near Lakewood in Walton County
Geographic center: 12 miles northwest of Brooksville in Hernando County
Coastline: 1,197 miles
Tidal shoreline: 2,276 miles
Beaches: 825 miles
Rivers, streams and waterways: Over 11,000 miles
Longest river: St. Johns, 273 miles
Largest lake: Lake Okeechobee at 730 square miles; Lake Okeechobee is the second largest freshwater lake in the contiguous 48 states of the United States
Largest county: Palm Beach at 2,578 square miles
Smallest county: Union at 245 square miles
Number of lakes greater than 10 acres: Approximately 7,700
Number of first-magnitude springs: 33; more first-magnitude springs than any other state
Number of islands greater than 10 acres: approximately 4,500, only Alaska has more

Source: *myflorida.com*

or less (downsizing) than the selling price of the current residence. The transferred SOH benefits apply to all taxes, including school taxes, on the new homestead.

Upsizing

If upsizing to a home of equal or greater "just" (market) value, the homestead owner can transfer 100 percent of the SOH benefit to the new homestead, up to $500,000 of transferred benefit. For example, suppose a homeowner sells a home with a just value/ market value of $400,000 that has a capped assessed value of $250,000. The accumulated SOH benefit is the difference, $150,000 ($400,000 - $250,000). If the homeowner purchases a new home for $600,000 (upsizing), then the entire accumulated SOH benefit can be applied so that the new capped assessed value of the newly acquired residence is now $450,000 ($600,000 - $150,000).

Downsizing

If downsizing to a home with a lower just value, the homestead owner can transfer a percentage of the accumulated SOH benefit to the new home. The percentage, applied to the prior capped assessed value, is determined by dividing the new just value by the old just value. In the example above, suppose the homeowner downsized to a home purchased for $300,000. The new just value of $300,000 divided by the old just value of $400,000 is 75 percent. To calculate the new home's capped value, apply the 75 percent to the prior capped value of $250,000 to yield $187,500. Stated another way, if you subtract 75 percent of the accumulated SOH benefit of $150,000 ($112,500) from the $300,000 value of the new homestead, you end up with $187,500 as the capped assessed value of the new home.

Split Ownership

If two or more people own multiple homesteads and are moving into only one new homestead, they can transfer an SOH benefit

Portability of Accumulated SOH Benefit

House Sold

Selling Price
$400,000

Just/Fair Market Value:
$400,000

SOH Exempt Benefit:
$150,000

Capped Assessed Value:
$250,000
($400,000 - $150,000)

(Upsizing)
House Purchased

Purchase Price
$600,000

Just/Fair Market Value:
$600,000

Applied SOH Exempt
Benefit (100%):
$150,000

New Home Assessed Value:
$450,000
($600,000 - $150,000)

(Downsizing)
House Purchased

Purchase Price
$300,000

Just/Fair Market Value:
$300,000

Applied SOH Exempt
* Benefit (75%):
$112,500 (75% of $150,000)

New Home Assessed Value:
$187,500
($300,000 - $112,500)

$$* \frac{\text{Market Value of New Home}}{\text{Market Value of Prior Home}} = 75\%$$

from one of the former homesteads up to a maximum of $500,000 of benefit.

If two or more people jointly own a homestead and are moving into more than one homestead, they must divide the value of their SOH benefit among the new homesteads based on the number of owners of the prior homestead. The total amount of transferable benefits is capped at $500,000.

Recapture Rule

Eloquently explained by the Pinellas County Property Appraiser's office, "If you have the Save Our Homes cap on your property and your just market value decreases, your assessed value will still increase by the annual cap rate until it reaches the just market value. If the just market value decreases below the assessed value, the assessed value will decrease until the two values are the same. This does not mean that you have lost your Save Our Homes cap. The cap is still on the property and will limit future increases of the assessed value." The chart below illustrates the relationship between the just market value and assessed value for a hypothetical property over several years.

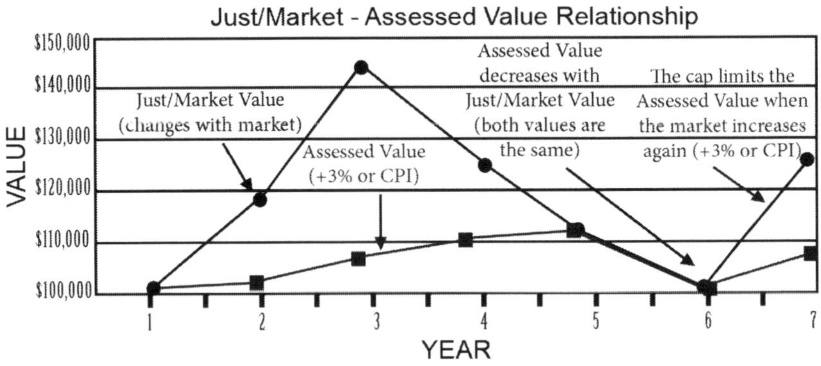

View a larger version of the chart above and find additional useful information on the Florida Save Our Homes benefit at www.pcpao.org/SOH.html.

Change of Ownership

Notwithstanding the provisions of the Florida Constitutional SOH Amendment discussed previously, any time a Florida home undergoes a change of ownership, a reassessment may be required to determine the fair market value as of January 1st of the year following the change. That could present a trap for the unwary. Florida statute defines a "change of ownership" to include any sale, foreclosure or transfer of legal or beneficial title to any person. However, exceptions include transfers between spouses, between legal and equitable title and after the change of ownership if the same person is entitled to the homestead exemption as was previously entitled (e.g., transferring the homestead to your revocable living trust).

The addition of a family member to the deed of a homestead property (e.g., a mother adding a daughter to the title) is not covered by the above exemptions and, thus, the tax clock would reset and start ticking all over again. Likewise, the transfer of a homestead to certain irrevocable trusts could cause a problem.

For example, transferring your home to a qualified personal residence trust (see *Chapter 4: Estate Planning for Florida Residents*), where title to the home passes to one or more of your children after a term of years has elapsed, may cause a reassessment at the end of the term of the trust, even if you continue to live in the home. With proper legal advice, you may be able to avoid these potential traps and retain your exemption.

Homestead Protections

Subject to the discussion about federal law below, your Florida homestead provides a constitutional protection from creditors. It means that, in general, your home cannot be sold against your will to satisfy the claims of your creditors. Homestead protection extends to the full value of your home and up to one-half acre of land within city limits and 160 contiguous acres outside a municipality. The protection from creditors is found in Article X, Section 4, of the Florida Constitution, which reads, in part:

> *There shall be exempt from forced sale under process of any court, and no judgment, decree or execution shall be a lien thereon, except for the payment of taxes and assessments thereon, obligations contracted for the purchase, improvement or repair thereof, or obligations contracted for house, field or other labor performed on the realty, the following property owned by a natural person: (1) A homestead, ...*

The Florida Supreme Court has been very protective of homestead property. In only very limited circumstances has the Court allowed a creditor to reach a homestead, such as permitting an equitable lien where funds obtained through fraud or other wrongful conduct could be traced directly to investment in the homestead. However, the Florida Supreme Court specifically ruled that transfer of nonexempt assets into an exempt homestead, even with the intent to hinder, delay or defraud creditors, does not allow a creditor to overcome the exemption and impose a lien on homestead property.

FLORIDA'S SPIRIT FLIES

Reprinted with permission of www.Bigstock.com

Florida's flag became official in 1900. Florida's flag has a diagonal red cross on a white field with the state seal in the center. The flag is based on the Confederate battle flag, which in turn was inspired by the cross of St. Andrew. The seal in the center illustrates a Seminole woman scattering flowers, the sun with many rays, palm trees, a sailing steamboat, the land and the water.

Source: *www.worldflags101.com*

Furthermore, the courts in Florida have been very generous in preventing forced sales of all sorts of home ownership, such as cooperative apartments, certain types of mobile homes or motor coaches and even some types of house boats.

In most cases, the homestead protection (from the homeowner's creditors) passes to the surviving spouse or heirs of the owner. This protection can provide a significant benefit to families if the homestead owner had substantial medical bills prior to death or if the deceased owner was involved in an accident for which the estate might be exposed to liability. Note two important points: 1.) the owner's homestead exemption protects the home against the owner's creditors, not the creditors of the surviving spouse or heirs and 2.) the extension of protection against the owner's creditors to the owner's spouse and heirs does not apply to residences that cannot be ordinarily treated as interests in real estate, such as cooperative apartments and mobile homes.

Homestead and Federal Law

Although Florida is very generous with its homestead asset protection laws, it is not always clear that the protection will apply when the creditor involved is the federal government or a creditor's claim is made in federal bankruptcy court. For example, a Florida homestead is not exempt from federal tax liens.

Furthermore, because of the Bankruptcy Abuse Prevention and Consumer Protection Act of 2005, newcomers to Florida will find that their home may not qualify for full protection right away if they are involved in a bankruptcy and have not resided in Florida for 1,215 days (approximately three years and four months) prior to filing a bankruptcy petition. Under the 2005 law, the homestead exemption is limited to $125,000 of equity if your homestead was acquired less than 1,215 days prior to a bankruptcy filing. This is true unless the homestead was acquired through an exempt rollover of proceeds from a prior exempt Florida residence and the combined holding period for the new and old exempt residences is 1,215 days.

However, after the waiting period, Florida's unlimited exemption amount on your homestead will apply.

The 2005 bankruptcy law also contains provisions designed to prevent the conversion of nonexempt assets into exempt homestead property if such conversion is done with the intent to hinder, delay or defraud creditors. In such a case, the value of the homestead is reduced by the value of such converted property if the conversion took place during the ten-year period preceding the filing of bankruptcy. This includes a substantial reduction in any outstanding mortgage to avoid current or reasonably foreseeable creditors. Moreover, none of the homestead is exempt if the debtor is convicted of a felony in conjunction with an abusive filing (as determined by the bankruptcy court) or the debtor owes a debt related to any of the following:

- A violation of federal or state securities laws,
- The purchase of registered securities through fraud, deceit or manipulation and
- Any criminal act, intentional tort or willful or reckless misconduct that caused serious physical injury or death in the preceding five years.

There is an exception to the complete non-exemption of the homestead of a debtor if the home is "reasonably necessary for the support of the debtor and any dependent." In this case, the exemption would be $125,000 of equity in the homestead.

Total Exemption of Homestead from Taxation

Real estate used and owned as a homestead by a quadriplegic, paraplegic or other totally and permanently disabled person who must use a wheelchair for mobility or is legally blind, is exempt from *ad valorem* (real estate) taxation. The applicant must produce a certificate of this disability from two unrelated and professionally licensed Florida physicians. Except for quadriplegics, who are exempt, the income of all persons residing at the homestead

Hurricane Facts

The Atlantic hurricane season, which affects Florida, runs for six months, from June 1 to November 30. Local TV stations and newspapers provide hurricane tracking maps, preparedness guides, seminars and regular forecasts so it is easy to be prepared. The National Hurricane Center's website, www.nhc.noaa.gov, provides the very latest information if a storm should develop.

Florida's first Weather Bureau Station opened in Miami in 1911. The National Hurricane Center has satellite offices located in six Florida cities and employs over 5,000 people worldwide.

In 2005, seven major hurricanes hit areas in or around Florida. There was much speculation that global warming was ushering in a new era in high hurricane activity for the Florida region. In 2017, most of the entire state of Florida experienced damage and lost electricity during Hurricane Irma, which landed in Collier County as a Category 4 storm. New Florida residents should educate themselves on what to do during a "tropical storm watch," a "hurricane watch" and a "hurricane warning."

The table below shows that the frequency of hurricanes of category 3 or greater in the continental U.S.

Time Period	Hurricanes of Category >3
1901-1920	11
1921-1940	13
1941-1960	19
1961-1980	10
1981-2000	9
2001-2017	10

Source: *National Hurricane Center*

(including Social Security benefits) cannot exceed an income ceiling determined yearly by the Florida Department of Revenue.

Further, real estate used and owned as a homestead by an American veteran—honorably discharged with a service-connected medical condition that resulted in total, permanent disability—is exempt from *ad valorem* taxation. The applicant must have a letter from the U.S. government or U.S. Department of Veteran Affairs confirming the disability. The veteran must be a permanent resident of Florida prior to January 1 of the tax year for which the exemption is claimed.

For details, call the property appraiser's office for the Florida county in which you are considering acquiring a new home. You can find a list of all Florida county property appraisers, including contact information, at www.floridarevenue.com.

Protection for a Spouse and Children

If you claim a Florida homestead, Florida law gives your spouse and minor children a special right in the home against your attempt to convey or encumber that home. Thus, even if the home is purchased in the sole name of a husband or wife (or a revocable living trust established by a husband or wife), when the home is mortgaged or resold, the lender or buyer will require one of the following:

- The signature of the other spouse on the mortgage, deed and/or conveying documents;
- A written waiver of homestead rights by the other spouse; or
- A statement on the deed confirming the property is not the homestead of the person signing the conveying document so there is no question of a violation of a spouse's homestead rights and, therefore, no potential cloud on the title.

For estate planning purposes, the homestead residence in Florida may be the most difficult asset to transfer freely. The general rule is that when a homestead is owned solely by one spouse and that spouse dies, the surviving spouse obtains a legal life estate (the right to possess and use the home for the remainder of his or her life) with a remainder interest going to the owner's lineal descendants.

Specifically, Article X, Section 4(c), of the Florida Constitution states:

> *The homestead shall not be subject to devise (transfer) if the owner is survived by a spouse or minor child, except the homestead may be devised to the owner's spouse if there be no minor child. The owner of homestead real estate, joined by the spouse if married, may alienate the homestead by mortgage, sale or gift and, if married, may, by deed, transfer the title to an estate by the entirety with the spouse ...*

For example, assume you are married and currently live in a state other than Florida. You own a Florida home that you have used as your vacation home. In a will, you leave the Florida home to your children from a prior marriage. In this case, the Florida home is not your homestead and can be freely transferred. However, if you move into the Florida home, declare Florida as your domicile and your spouse does not waive homestead rights before your death, your spouse will have a life estate in the home and your children from your prior marriage will receive the home only upon your spouse's death, regardless of what your will says.

Loss of Homestead Exemption

The rental of a dwelling previously claimed to be a homestead for tax purposes constitutes abandonment of the dwelling as a homestead resulting in loss of the homestead exemption. Abandonment of a homestead after January 1 of any year does not affect the homestead exemption for tax purposes for that particular year.

When, Where and How to File for the Exemption

To qualify for the homestead exemption in a certain year, you must have legal or equitable title to the property and reside in the property as your primary residence as of January 1; that is, you must have established your Florida domicile prior to January 1. Furthermore, you must apply in person (or by mail, if permitted in your county) prior to March 1 at the county appraiser's office or one of the satellite locations designated by the county appraiser throughout the county in which the property is located. The schedule indicating the satellite locations for filing for the exemption is usually published each year in the local newspaper or you may call the property appraiser's office in the county where your home is located for information.

If you were unable to take title to your property by the first of January and/or you did not establish Florida domicile in the prior year, you will not qualify for the homestead exemption in that particular year; thus, you will have to wait until the following year to establish your homestead exemption. However, most Florida county offices accept pre-filed applications ("early filing") for the following tax year throughout the current year so that you might avoid long lines at the regular filing times.

You must produce certain documents, dated prior to January 1 of the tax year for which you are applying for the exemption, to verify your qualification for the exemption. These documents typically include the following:

- A copy of your Declaration of Domicile that was filed with the clerk of the circuit court;
- A recorded deed or copy of the tax bill to your Florida home in your name—as evidence of ownership;
- Social Security numbers for all owners (i.e., for you and your spouse if the home is in both your names);
- Your Florida driver license. If you don't drive, you must show a Florida ID card issued by the Department of

Florida Day Trip Ideas

Florida is a great state to explore. With a full tank of gas and the willingness to be spontaneous, there are countless destinations to fill every weekend of the year.

Southeast Florida

Fairchild Tropical Botanic Garden: From rare tropical plants and a lush "rainforest" to a butterfly garden, Fairchild has set the bar for botanical gardens. A must for plant and flower lovers.

Southwest Florida

The Peace River: Camp, canoe, fish, hike or search for shark teeth. Voted the best river in Florida, 12 years in a row.

Central Florida

Merritt Island National Wildlife Refuge: Kayak through these bioluminescent waters and streaks of blue-green lights will catch your eye. Everything under the water glows.

Northeast Florida

Fernandina Beach: Experience horseback riding like never before. This is one of the few places in Florida where you can ride horseback on the beach.

Florida Panhandle

Florida Caverns State Park: The only park in Florida to offer cave tours to the public. These dry caves date back thousands of years to when Native Americans would use them for shelter.

Source: *Visit Florida*

Highway Safety and Motor Vehicles;

- Your Florida vehicle registration;
- Your Voter Information Card for the county in which your home is located;
- Your resident alien "green" card if you are not a U.S. citizen; and
- If your property is held in a trust, a complete copy of the trust agreement—so that eligibility of the trust to qualify for the homestead exemption can be determined.

A sample application for homestead exemption (Form DR 501) is included in Appendix B2.

QUESTIONS AND ANSWERS

Florida Homestead

Q: Will I lose my Homestead Exemption if I add someone to my deed?

A: Adding names to the ownership of your home normally does not change your Homestead Exemption BUT you may lose all or part of the protection your property receives from the Save Our Homes (SOH) assessment limitation or "cap." The SOH cap keeps the assessed value (not the taxes) of your home from increasing more than 3% per year as long as you maintain your Homestead Exemption. A loss of protection from the SOH cap will increase the amount of property taxes you pay.

Q: Will I lose my Save Our Homes cap if I add someone to my deed?

A: Maybe, depending on how you own the property (the "tenancy") and if the new owner files for Homestead Exemption on your property. "Tenancy" is the term used to describe the way property is owned, the relationship between the owners and what happens to the property when an owner dies. The most common forms of tenancy are: Tenancy by the Entireties, Joint Tenants with Right of Survivorship and Tenants in Common. If two or more people own property with a homestead exemption, the type of tenancy that appears on the deed can have an effect on the "Save Our Homes" provision and, ultimately, on the amount of taxes that are owed.

- If the new owner is your spouse or someone who is legally or naturally dependent on you, he or she must apply for homestead exemption. Your current Save Our Homes cap will not be adjusted.
- If the new owner is a joint tenant with right of survivorship and he or she DOES NOT apply for Homestead Exemption, your SOH cap WILL NOT be adjusted. Alternatively, if the new owner is a joint tenant with right of survivorship and DOES apply for Homestead Exemption, your SOH cap WILL be adjusted to market value and start anew the following year. In future years, the SOH cap will protect 100% of the property.

One Important Note! If the new owner is living with you and intends to make the property his or her permanent residence, it may make more sense to apply for the new Homestead Exemption now rather than waiting until a later date. Your Homestead Exemption and SOH cap protect only you and not the new owner. In the future, if you no longer reside in this home, the new owner will have to apply at that time and the property value and taxes will most certainly be much higher than they are now.

- If the new owner is a tenant in common and DOES NOT apply for homestead exemption, your SOH cap WILL BE adjusted to protect only your proportionate or "percent" interest in the property. The "percent" interest of any owner who does not have homestead exemption will be assessed at market value each year. Alternatively, if the new owner DOES apply for Homestead Exemption, your

SOH cap WILL BE adjusted to market value and start anew the following year.

Q: Can someone "inherit" the Save Our Homes value when inheriting a family-owned property?

A: Probably not. In general, a person cannot "inherit" another's homestead exemption or Save Our Homes cap benefit even if he or she inherits the property. When property changes ownership after the death of the homesteaded owner, the decedent's exemption is removed at the end of the year. The new owner must file for his or her own exemption once he or she has ownership of the home. There are two exceptions which allow someone to "inherit" an existing Save Our Homes cap benefit:

- A surviving spouse may retain the existing Save Our Homes cap—even if the survivor was not previously on the title—so long as the surviving spouse subsequently files for homestead exemption; and
- The existing Save Our Homes cap may be retained if the person inheriting the property—or being granted a life estate or beneficial rights under a trust—was naturally or legally a dependent of the decedent AND was permanently residing on the property at the time of the decedent's death (see: Section 193.155 (3), Florida Statutes).

In all other instances, the person inheriting the property must file for a new Homestead Exemption.

Q: Can I "undo" or cancel a deed that is already recorded?

A: If the wording of your current deed has consequences that you did not intend, you may want to consider a corrective deed. Please consult an attorney, title company or other real estate professional to help you prepare your corrective deed. The Property Appraiser's office cannot advise you, since there are many serious considerations that go beyond how homestead exemption is calculated, including income and estate tax consequences. We recommend that you never attempt to change your deed without the help of a professional.

Q: Are there other ways of transferring my property for estate planning that will not disturb my Homestead Exemption or SOH cap?

A: Two methods of transferring your property will, in most cases, keep your Homestead Exemption and SOH intact: reserve a Life Estate for yourself or transfer your property to your trust. Please consult your attorney or estate-planning professional before attempting either option.

If you transfer your property to a trust, your attorney should know that three criteria are required in order for your Homestead Exemption and SOH cap to remain intact:

- You as the homestead owner must have beneficial or equitable title to real property. In other words, you must be the trustee or beneficiary of the trust. If you are the beneficiary but not the trustee, your interest must be in REAL property, not PERSONAL property.
- You must have a present possessory interest in the property. Simply, you must have the right to live there.
- The deed that transfers the property into the trust must be recorded.

Q: Can my attorney contact the county appraiser's office to get questions answered?

A: Absolutely! You, your attorney or estate-planning professional are encouraged to call the Florida Property Appraiser Exemptions Department in the county where you reside with any questions.

The above questions and answers courtesy of the Pinellas County Florida Property Appraiser, Mike Twitty and his staff from its website: www.pcpao.org/SOH.html

Please consult your attorney or estate-planning professional. The above information is provided only to help you understand homestead exemption and does not constitute legal advice.

"JEROME IS RETIRED, BUT HE STILL WORKS IN ORDER to AFFORD BEING RETIRED."

There is only one success: to be able to spend your life in your own way.
–Christopher Morley

CHAPTER 4

ESTATE PLANNING FOR FLORIDA RESIDENTS

Florida has no state income tax, state gift tax, state inheritance tax and, effectively, no state estate tax. Florida actually does have a state estate tax as a part of its laws; however, the Economic Growth and Tax Relief Reconciliation Act of 2001 eliminated the credit for payment of state estate taxes. Many states, including Florida, have estate tax laws that provide that the state estate tax is equal to the credit allowed on the federal estate tax return for payment of state estate taxes. When the federal government eliminated the tax credit, Florida's estate tax was effectively eliminated.

A number of states, in response to this loss of revenue, have "decoupled" from the old arrangement and have enacted state estate and/or inheritance taxes that are independent of the federal estate tax. While Florida has not decoupled, many new Florida residents have been motivated to make the move to Florida in order to avoid paying onerous state estate and inheritance taxes in their former northern states.

Importantly, in order to pass a new state tax in Florida, a 60 percent affirmative vote by the citizens of the state is required. As such, it is unlikely that the residents of Florida will enact a new tax upon themselves.

Estate Tax Exposure on Non-Florida Real Estate

The absence of estate, gift or generation-skipping transfer (GST) tax in Florida is good news if you are planning on becoming a permanent Florida resident. But if, after you become a Florida resident, you still own property (typically, real estate) in your former state at your death, there may be ramifications if that state has decoupled from the federal estate tax system or has established a separate state estate tax. Depending on the value of your property in another state, it is possible that your former state will tax that property at your death—even if no federal estate tax is due.

Some decoupled states have set a level of exemption from their state estate tax that is well below the federal estate tax exemption. For example, in Massachusetts, the state exemption is currently only $1M. So, if you own real estate in Massachusetts at the time of your death with a value in excess of the state exemption amount, the state will assess a tax on your estate. Furthermore, it may not matter if

WHAT'S A CONCH?

Florida's state shell is the horse conch, a mollusk with a large pale orange shell. Though today the shellfish is rare, there are many conchs on dry land. "Conch" is a term used to indicate a native of the Keys, especially Key West. Originally, though, it described Bahamians of European descent. One of the theories on the origin of the term is that the Europeans ate a great deal of conch. Eventually, the term evolved to include Europeans in the Florida Keys and the name stuck.

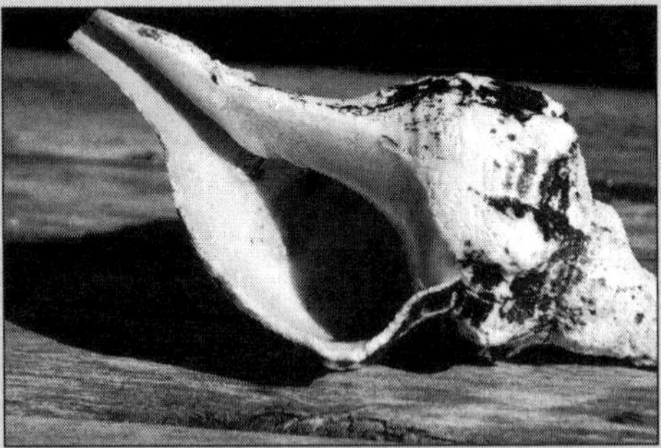

Reprinted with permission of www.Bigstock.com

Source: *The Florida Keys: A History of the Pioneers by John Viele.*

you are married. Even if you die first and pass all or a portion of that real estate to your spouse in a typical bypass (B) trust designed to use your federal estate tax exemption while benefiting your spouse and family, the trust may not protect your estate from state estate tax.

Fundamental Estate Planning

For a well-planned estate—one that avoids probate, takes care of you in the event of your incapacity and helps confirm your status as a Florida resident—you should have the following basic estate-planning documents:

- Living Will
- Health Care Surrogate Designation
- Health Insurance Portability and Accountability Act (HIPAA) authorization for release of medical information
- Revocable Living Trust
- Pour-Over Will
- Durable Power of Attorney

Living Will

A living will is a document in which you state whether life-sustaining procedures should be used to prolong your life if you are terminally ill, have an end-stage condition or are in a persistent vegetative state. Florida, like most states, has specifically approved the use of living wills by statute.

With improvements in medical technology, the possibility of prolonging life can go far beyond what most people have ever imagined. Yet many people are unwilling to suffer the loss of their dignity—and possibly their life savings, as the necessary payment for prolonging their lives—when death is otherwise imminent. They simply want to retain the right to control decisions regarding

Destination Theme Parks

In the 1960s, Walt Disney came to Florida in search of a site for a model idealized working community. On October 1, 1971, Walt Disney World opened and was followed soon after by EPCOT (an acronym for his Experimental Prototype City of Tomorrow). This subsequently expanded into a larger network of theme parks, resort hotels and communities that now exist on the Disney property.

When President Kennedy launched the space program, NASA laid claim to a huge parcel of land on the northeast coast for the John F. Kennedy Space Center. The center offers IMAX theaters, the Astronaut Hall of Fame, museums devoted to space exploration and space simulation rides.

Busch Entertainment Corp., the family entertainment division of Anheuser-Busch, runs SeaWorld and Busch Gardens. Busch Gardens, located in Tampa, opened in 1959 as an African theme park. You can explore African wildlife, along with many roller coasters. This park also features the famous Budweiser Clydesdales. SeaWorld, located in Orlando, opened in 1973 as a fun park featuring many sea creatures.

NASCAR fans can enjoy a live test-drive experience at Richard Petty Driving Experience. Featured at three locations, Miami, Orlando and Daytona, you can experience the thrill of riding in a racecar with a professional driver at 165 miles per hour.

Created in 1946, Weeki Wachee Springs is a water park that will supply fun for the whole family. This park was built on a spring in Brooksville and features Buccaneer Bay water park, canoe and glass bottom boat rides, snorkeling, scuba diving and an underwater theater with mermaid shows.

Source: *Visit Florida*

their medical care, including the withholding or withdrawing of life-sustaining procedures.

Florida's living will laws contain safeguards to ensure peace of mind, such as a requirement that two physicians examine the patient and determine that recovery is no longer likely before life-sustaining treatments may be withdrawn. If you sign a living will, you can revoke it at any time by destroying it, directing its destruction or by signing a written revocation.

Health Care Surrogate Designation

A designation of health care surrogate is a document, authorized under Florida laws, that allows you to choose a person to make your medical decisions for you if you cannot. It covers decisions on issues that may arise before you are terminally ill, such as operations, transfusions, nursing care and various medical treatments. Florida law has the effect of empowering your agent to make virtually any type of health care decision you could make for yourself.

Release of Medical Information

The Health Insurance Portability and Accountability Act (HIPAA) authorization for release of information helps ensure your agent (i.e., a family member) will have the right to obtain your medical records to share with health care professionals should the need arise. The HIPAA authorization can be a separate document or may be incorporated in other documents, such as your health care surrogate designation.

Revocable Living Trust

Whether you die in Florida or elsewhere, you should have a proper estate plan that includes instructions on how you want your assets distributed at death. You could accomplish this with a will but it is often better accomplished using a revocable living trust (RLT).

A will is only operative at your death, whereas an RLT goes far beyond a will by providing instructions about how you want your affairs to be handled while you are alive and well or if you become incapacitated. Your RLT includes instructions on how you would like your property and financial affairs managed and it forms the foundation of an effective estate plan.

In most RLTs, you, as the trust maker (or grantor), are the trustee of your trust during your lifetime. As trustee, you continue to manage your assets and file your federal income tax returns as you always have. In addition, you may transfer assets to and from the trust whenever you desire. You can name your spouse as co-trustee or as a successor trustee—the person who would take over if you resign, become disabled or die.

An RLT offers two major benefits to you and your family that cannot be achieved with a will:

- Avoiding probate when the trust is properly funded and
- Providing instructions in the event of your incapacity.

Avoiding Probate

The most talked about advantage of an RLT is the avoidance of probate. Many people mistakenly think that they avoid probate by having a will. Just the opposite is true. Relying on a will to dispose of assets guarantees probate because one purpose of probate is to prove the validity of the will. A properly drafted RLT, funded with your assets during your lifetime, on the other hand, can help you minimize or even avoid probate. There are numerous reasons why a person may wish to avoid probate, even in Florida where the probate process is considered to be fairly simple. Following are some of those reasons:

Cost: The costs associated with probating your estate, including personal representative fees, attorney fees and court costs, can amount to 6 percent or more of your gross estate in Florida and, depending on the state in which you are domiciled at your death, the costs can be much greater than in Florida. The cost of preparing a typical RLT is usually very small in comparison to the costs of probating your estate—which would be the result of dying with only a will. When properly funded, an RLT can completely avoid probate and the associated costs.

Time: Probate takes time and it can easily be a year or more before the process is completed. In the absence of tax issues, with an RLT, there is virtually no waiting because the trust does not die; only the grantor does.

State lines: Wills do not cross state lines well. If you have property, such as real estate, in more than one state, your heirs will likely face ancillary probate in each additional state where your property is located. This can add substantially to the costs and time delays. With a properly funded RLT, probate is often unnecessary, regardless of where the properties are located.

Public: Certain documents in probate matters are public records. An RLT is private; the public will know virtually nothing about your estate and the details of the inheritance your heirs receive.

Contests: Wills are often easier to contest than trusts. You may believe that your heirs won't challenge your will but, when people die, heirs may begin quarreling with each other. You cannot be sure that no one will contest your wishes. As a client once remarked, "If you really want to get to know someone, share an inheritance with that person." An RLT is harder to dispute because it is a living document and usually funded by you before you die. Also, with you as trustee of your RLT, there leaves little doubt about your true intentions. With an RLT, typically, you may make any changes you desire while you are alive and competent. If an heir believes he or she has a basis for a lawsuit, the heir would have to bring suit him- or herself rather than simply raising the issue in an already-established probate proceeding.

Providing for Disability

The second major reason for having an RLT, and one that many experts consider more important than avoiding probate, is having your wishes carried out in the event you become incapacitated. The fact is you are four to six times more likely to become disabled than to die in the next year. Therefore, it is important to prepare in advance so that you and your loved ones can be cared for in the manner you desire during your incapacity.

Many people feel that they have adequately planned for incapacity because they have a durable power of attorney. A durable power of attorney is a legal document that gives the person of your choice the right to act in your place regarding all financial matters. Unfortunately, some financial institutions won't recognize a durable power of attorney, especially if the document is old and does not contain language dictated by state law. Even though Florida has a law that requires a financial institution to honor a durable power of attorney, if the document is not drafted in accordance with the Florida statute, problems may arise.

An RLT, on the other hand, allows you to choose, in detail, how you want your affairs handled if you become incapacitated and lets you set the priority of your wishes. Financial institutions are more likely to recognize and follow RLT instructions when the grantor of the trust is disabled or incapacitated.

If you have neither a durable power of attorney nor an RLT and you become incapacitated, your spouse or your children would have to go through the legal process of guardianship. And although the probate court would most likely appoint your spouse (or adult family member if you have no spouse) to manage your affairs, he or she would have to report annually to the court and your affairs would be subject to legal costs and the red tape of the court system. Fortunately, you can easily avoid all this with an RLT; your successor trustee (typically your spouse) manages your affairs from the moment you become disabled without any legal proceedings or court intervention.

Planning for Estate Taxes

An RLT can provide you with benefits you cannot receive with a will and typically includes your instructions for minimizing federal estate taxes. A married person who leaves everything to his or her spouse in what is known as an "I love you" will avoids any federal estate tax at the death of the first spouse because of the unlimited federal marital deduction (no tax on assets left to your spouse). However, at the surviving spouse's death, the property owned by that spouse, including the property inherited from the first spouse to die, is then subjected to the federal estate tax. The problem with this simple arrangement is that, without post-mortem estate tax planning and filing an estate tax return, it could waste the *applicable exclusion amount* of the first spouse to die. With a properly worded RLT, it is possible to preserve your exemption by leaving the exemption amount either directly to others (e.g., your children) or to a trust that is set up to benefit your family, including your spouse.

A common arrangement involves the use of an RLT that splits into two trusts upon the first death: a marital trust (often known as a qualified terminable interest property (QTIP) trust or the A trust) and a family trust (often referred to as a bypass trust, a credit shelter trust or simply a B trust). The family trust preserves the applicable exclusion amount of the first spouse to die while providing for the needs of the surviving spouse and the marital trust preserves the unlimited marital deduction for the balance of the estate.

SNOW BIRDS

Common brown pelicans remain in Florida all year. The endangered white pelicans, like many of our seasonal residents, are sometimes referred to as "snow birds" because they arrive in Florida during the cold northern winter months and return to their northern homes for the spring and summer.

Reprinted with permission of Bigstock.com

Protecting Your Heirs

An RLT also offers flexibility as to how you leave your assets to help protect your heirs. You may, for example, pass assets to your heirs with certain strings attached. By doing so, you can control how and when your assets are distributed after your death.

For example, some years ago, a Florida resident had a son who was a "deadhead" (i.e., a follower of the rock group known as the Grateful Dead). The son would follow the group from concert to concert and sell tie-dye T-shirts to make enough money to eat and travel. The parents were quite wealthy but were worried about their son's lifestyle and propensity for spending money. So, in their RLT, they arranged for their son to receive his inheritance through a trust that provided him with two dollars from their estate for every dollar he legitimately earned. This type of trust is commonly referred to as an *incentive trust*.

Many professional planners believe that no one should leave anything of any consequence to anyone outright. Instead, everything should be left in *asset protection trusts*. By leaving assets in trust for children, you can protect them in a way they cannot do for themselves.

THE CITRUS SIDE OF FLORIDA

Florida has a long and profitable history of orange juice production that began during World War II when concentrated juice was invented. The process removed the water from the juice so it could be stored and re-hydrated later. The industry really took off with frozen concentrate and now it's a multibillion dollar industry. Most Florida oranges are grown in the southern two-thirds of the state, out of the reach of frosts. The height of the season is December through May when a trip to a local fruit stand will yield fresh oranges and a variety of other succulent citrus.

Source: *myflorida.com; floridajuice.com*

For example, your RLT could provide for each child to receive his or her inheritance in trust, allowing the child to serve as his or her own trustee or as a co-trustee. As a trustee, each child or, for that matter, any of your heirs can manage the funds however he or she desires. However, by retaining everything in trust, you may successfully prevent an unwanted creditor from a failed business venture, an overzealous litigator (e.g., as a result of an auto accident) or even a child's spouse or ex-spouse from ever gaining access to the assets in the trust.

In essence, you may accomplish two very important goals: you will have 1.) set the assets aside, allowing each child to manage and benefit from his or her own share and 2.) preserved the assets from successful attack by a third party.

When offered the opportunity to provide asset protection for their children, parents are sometimes concerned that, by leaving assets in trust, they are over-controlling their children. This is a legitimate concern that must be reviewed with a qualified attorney. Keeping assets in trust for children should never be a question if the children can serve as trustees. This plan will provide them with significant flexibility and control. This simple arrangement should be compared with a more elaborate design involving co-trustees or independent trustees. Though more complicated, the latter arrangement arguably provides more protection from creditors and from the beneficiary himself or herself than the former.

Another issue you need to face involves whether to allow your children to leave the assets remaining in their respective trusts to anyone they desire at their deaths (for example, to their spouses—who might remarry and choose to disinherit your grandchildren) or whether to restrict them to leaving these assets to your descendants.

Furthermore, by including generation skipping provisions in your RLT (though you do not really skip anyone, except the IRS), you can also protect your children and grandchildren from additional layers of estate tax on a substantial portion of the assets that remain in trust at death. This protection can last up to 360 years in Florida. However, there is a limit on how much you can leave in trust that skips the IRS.

In summary, the RLT represents a very flexible tool that will allow you to remain in control of your estate while providing a way to avoid probate, follow your wishes in the event of your disability, help save estate taxes, protect your heirs and avoid additional estate taxes at your children's deaths.

Funding Your RLT

To obtain the full benefits of having an RLT, it should be funded with virtually all your assets, with the notable exceptions of any retirement plan assets (such as an IRA, 401(k) and/or annuities) and, possibly, your Florida homestead. Funding involves the transfer of assets from your name to your name as trustee (or to some other trustee, if appropriate) of your RLT.

An annuity, IRA or typical qualified plan has its own beneficiary designation form and, therefore, would not be controlled by your will or trust unless one or more of those instruments names your trust as

GEOGRAPHY: CENTRAL FLORIDA

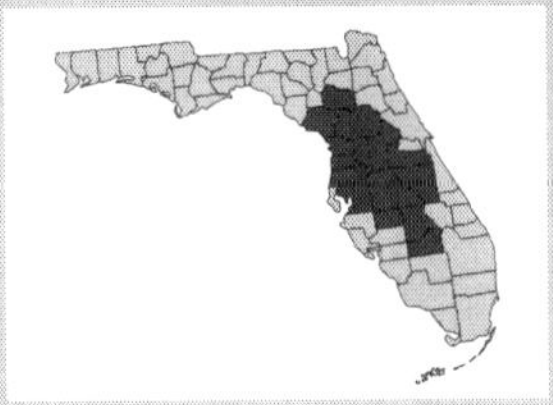

Central Florida stretches from Gainesville to Lake Okeechobee. Some of the major cities included in central Florida are Orlando, Lakeland, Ocala and Gainesville. Central Florida has few beaches, but hundreds of freshwater lakes that provide excellent bass fishing and freshwater springs, such as those showcased at Silver Springs. Horse lovers are sure to enjoy the rolling hills around Ocala where thoroughbred racehorses are raised. For urban pleasures, Orlando has a thriving nightlife scene and families flock to its many theme parks, including Disney World, Universal Studios and SeaWorld. Finally, Gainesville, home of the University of Florida Gators, offers a funky college town experience.

Facts About Central Florida

Orlando attracts more visitors than any other amusement park destination in the United States.

Gatorade was named for the University of Florida Gators where the drink was first developed.

Aviator Tony Jannus made history on January 1, 1914, when he flew the world's first scheduled passenger airline flight from St. Petersburg's downtown yacht basin to Tampa.

L. Neal Smith and his brother of Montverde developed the first Snapper riding lawn mower.

Plant City, the Winter Strawberry Capital of the World, once produced an 827 square foot, 6,000 pound cake on February 19, 1999, hosts an annual Strawberry Festival in late February.

Fort Meade is the oldest settlement in Polk County. It dates back to 1849 when a settlement grew around the U.S. Calvary fort during the Seminole Indian Wars.

Clearwater has the highest rate of lightning strikes per capita in the U.S.

The Fred Bear Museum in Gainesville is a tribute to the accomplishments of Fred Bear, a promoter of proper wildlife management and the founder of Bear Archery Company.

The Gainesville-Hawthorne Trail, a part of Florida's Rails to Trails program, attracts many outdoor enthusiasts to walk, cycle or ride horseback through its 17-mile length.

The Pinellas Trail, a 47-mile hiking/biking trail connecting St. Petersburg with central and north Pinellas County, is the longest urban linear trail in the eastern United States.

the beneficiary at your death. Also, by changing the ownership of a qualified plan, IRA or annuity to your trust, you may unnecessarily trigger income tax.

You should seek legal advice on whether to title your Florida homestead residence to your RLT, as your attorney may be concerned that you could lose valuable protection against creditors. In a case decided a few years ago by a federal bankruptcy court for the Middle District of Florida, the judge determined that the creditor exemption under Florida's Constitution for a homestead residence does not apply when the residence is held in an RLT. The reasoning behind the ruling was that a revocable living trust is not considered a *natural person* as defined in the Florida Constitution and, therefore, does not

Florida Parks & Monuments

Florida contains 160 state parks existing on more than 700,000 acres. The parks feature crystal-clear springs, miles of beaches, rivers, lakes and an abundance of wildlife and outdoor activities. Also, there are 33 state forests and seven park preserves in Florida. Five national monuments and memorials show Florida's history: Castillo de San Marcos, DeSoto, Fort Caroline, Fort Jefferson and Fort Matanzas. The architecture in these historic sites reveals the rich diversity of Florida's first European settlers.

Reprinted with permission of www.Bigstock.com

After a colorful history of occupation by the British and re-occupation by the Spanish, the oldest city in the United States, St. Augustine and the entire state of Florida was sold to America in 1821. In 1883, oil baron Henry Flagler restored St. Augustine and turned it into a winter resort.

Source: *Visit Florida*

meet the requirement under the Constitution that a homestead be owned by a natural person. Although this position has since been rejected by a number of courts, prudence suggests that you should consult with a qualified estate-planning attorney before transferring your homestead to an RLT.

Pour-Over Will

One of the most common mistakes in estate planning is failing to fund an RLT. Any asset that has not been placed in your name as trustee of your RLT will be subject to probate unless it is owned jointly or has a beneficiary designation. To ensure that all your individually owned assets end up in your trust containing your detailed instructions on the disposition of your assets at death, your attorney should arrange for you to execute a will that directs any assets not in your RLT to pour over into the trust. This is known as a *pour-over will.*

Durable Power of Attorney

A durable power of attorney is a document that allows you, as principal, to authorize another person (the attorney-in-fact or agent) to act on your behalf with respect to specified legal matters, even if you subsequently become incapacitated. This document names who will make decisions and lists the decision-making powers it confers. A special durable power of attorney for funding limits your agent's authority to the funding of assets into your revocable living trust and would typically be used in the event of your incapacity.

Life Insurance

Life insurance is a legal contract, referred to as a policy, which guarantees to pay a certain sum of money (the death benefit) to a specified person or entity (the beneficiary) when the insured dies. The policy remains in effect as long as its cost (the premium) has been paid according to the contractual provisions.

You can own a policy personally or have some other person or entity—such as a trust—own it instead. The owner controls the policy and has the legal right to name the beneficiary, change the beneficiary, cancel the policy and/or withdraw or borrow from the policy's cash value at any time. The owner is responsible for any tax consequences relating to the premium, cash value and death benefit.

Most people don't think of it this way but life insurance is actually risk sharing among a group of people with the common goal of providing money to beneficiaries when an insured party dies. It is somewhat like a lottery in that money is pooled to provide a benefit (death benefit) which, in the case of life insurance, goes to the beneficiaries of those who die while their contract is in force. Most Floridians purchase insurance because they love someone or something but life insurance can be used for many purposes, including:

- Providing financial security for loved ones
- Protecting future generations
- Paying estate taxes
- Replacing wealth
- Paying a debt, such as a mortgage
- Equalizing inheritance
- Purchasing an interest in a business
- Protecting a business
- Diversifying an investment portfolio
- Giving to charity
- Providing for retirement
- Replacing lost income
- Offsetting gifts to charity

- Making up for a bad investment
- Recovering the cost of a corporate obligation

Life insurance is often the only way to effectively provide for many of the above needs. In many cases, it is also the least expensive way. Life insurance is so versatile that it can provide benefits during life as well as after death. For example, in certain types of life insurance there is an accumulation of cash inside the policy from premium payments paid in excess of mortality charges and expenses. The policy owner can access this accumulation during his or her lifetime via withdrawals and/or policy loans. These withdrawals and loans are often tax-deferred and, if the policy is held to maturity, can be tax-free—allowing the full amount to be used for lifetime needs, such as retirement income, college educations and emergencies.

Life Settlement

If a life insurance policy is no longer needed or wanted, the policy can be *cashed in* to the insurance company for its current cash value, if any, or it can be sold in what is known as a life settlement transaction. The sale of insurance policies through a life settlement is a relatively new and fast-growing industry. Life settlement companies, often backed by hedge funds, pension funds and, in some cases, well-known financial institutions, act as *funders* and purchase policies for more than their current cash surrender value. The proceeds from a life settlement can be used for any number of purposes, including:

- To fund alternative financial products
- To pay off medical bills
- To offset increased living expenses
- To make gifts to family members
- To purchase a vacation home

- To buy a replacement policy with the same death benefit but lower premiums
- To buy a replacement policy with better guarantees
- To buy a replacement policy with the same premium but a larger death benefit

Virtually any type of policy from any carrier—including individual term (if the policy is convertible), whole and universal life, group, corporate-owned and policies held in irrevocable trusts—can be sold for more than the current cash value, for some percentage of the death benefit. The most attractive settlements are for policies with a death benefit of $500,000 or more, where the insured is over 65 years of age and has had a health change since the policy was issued. However, an insured does not have to be sick to qualify for a life settlement.

Florida Dinosaurs

Alligators, these iconic reptiles, have made a remarkable comeback from the endangered species list and now they are thriving in all 67 Florida counties. In fact, they are so plentiful that the Florida Fish and Wildlife Conservation Commission removed about 8,118 nuisance gators in 2016. The Commission issues a certain number of permits each year to control the population. It is illegal to feed or harass the alligators. At up to 14 feet in length and 1,000 pounds in weight, a mature alligator can be an awe-inspiring sight.

Reprinted with permission of www.Bigstock.com

Source: *Florida Fish and Wildlife Conservation Commission, myfwc.com*

Whatever your reason for terminating an existing policy, before you let your life insurance policy lapse or settle for the cash surrender value, you should check to see if a life settlement company will offer a better alternative. You can learn more about life insurance and life settlements for Florida residents online at www.fldfs.com or www.kilbournassociates.com.

Asset Protection Planning

Proper planning includes protecting your assets from unjust and unduly large judgments obtained by creditors. It is a prudent and, in some cases, necessary course of action, especially if you are wealthy—a characteristic that frequently makes people the target of gold-digging plaintiffs. By protecting your assets and reducing your liability exposure, potential plaintiffs are likely to either refrain from filing suit or settle early to save litigation costs and time.

Transferring your assets to a Revocable Living Trust (RLT) will *not* protect your assets from your creditors; however, there are several other entities, often used in estate and wealth planning, which could help provide asset protection. Three of the most common are the family limited partnership, the family limited liability company and the irrevocable trust.

Family Limited Partnerships

A family limited partnership (FLP) is a business entity formed among family members under state law (e.g., Florida statutes). Individuals contribute property to the partnership in exchange for limited or general partnership interests. General partnership interests, no matter how small, control the management of and distributions from the partnership, while limited partnership interests are generally passive and only receive income, if earned, at the direction and under the control of the general partner. While the general partner is liable for debts of the partnership, limited partners are protected from claims of partnership creditors because of the passive nature of the interests.

Owners of an FLP may enhance the asset protection benefits offered under Florida law by electing to form (or convert an existing FLP to) a limited liability partnership, which is a special form of limited partnership that limits the liability of the limited partners and the general partner, as well.

In the context of estate planning, a significant advantage of an FLP is that the fair market value of the limited partnership interests is typically less than the value of the underlying assets. This reflects the fact that limited partners do not have control and the interests are less marketable (often because of restrictions in the partnership agreement). Such *discounts* to the underlying value of the FLP frequently result in the limited partner interests being valued at as little as 65 percent of the underlying asset value, thereby reducing the base upon which gift or estate taxes are levied when the shares are given to loved ones during life or at death.

Family Limited Liability Companies

The family limited liability company (FLLC) is a type of hybrid business structure that is designed to provide the limited liability features of a corporation and the tax efficiencies and operational flexibility of a partnership. The FLLC is formed under state law among family members and is one of the easiest and least expensive forms of ownership to organize. It is a popular choice among families who are looking for asset protection and other benefits without the complication of a corporation.

Unlike an FLP where, under the laws of most states including Florida, the general partner (parents or other entity) is not protected from partnership liabilities, all owners of the shares of an FLLC, including the *manager(s)*, have limited liability for business debts.

Parents can transfer FLLC ownership interests, often at discount (so that they can make transfers that are larger than their gift tax exemptions might otherwise allow), in the form of non-voting, non-management interests to children and/or grandchildren (or trusts for their benefit) without relinquishing control.

Estate Planning Benefits of an FLP or FLLC

In estate planning, a family limited partnership (FLP) or family limited liability company (FLLC) is often used to enhance an efficient wealth transfer program. The use of either entity could accomplish the following:

- Provide centralized asset management for family assets;
- Provide the opportunity for significant discounts to the fair market value of any gifts you make, allowing you to give more, possibly as much as 50 to 75 percent more than your gift tax exemption would otherwise allow. The discounts (determined through valuations) result from a *lack of marketability and lack of control* relative to the gifted FLP or FLLC interests;
- Allow you to fund your FLP or FLLC with many types of assets, including stocks, bonds, real estate and cash;
- Allow you, as general partner of an FLP or managing member of an FLLC, to *charge* a reasonable management fee, which provides you with the option of earning a portion of the income produced by assets in the FLP or FLLC—before distributions are made on a pro-rata basis;
- Allow the appreciation of assets owned by the FLP or FLLC, to the extent given to family members (or trusts for their benefit), to occur outside your estate—free of gift or estate tax;
- Provide a way to consolidate multistate family real estate in one entity to avoid ancillary probate and potential domicile claims by a former state of residence; and/or
- Protect the assets placed inside the FLP or FLLC from attachment by individual creditors.

Irrevocable Trusts

A typical irrevocable trust (IRT) is a trust that you set up while you are alive for the benefit of others and that you normally cannot change. Depending on the type of trust, the trustee of an IRT may be someone other than you (the *grantor*) because the trust cannot be controlled by or benefit the grantor without the risk of having the value of the trust assets included in the grantor's estate for estate tax purposes. By transferring one or more assets to an IRT, you are making an irrevocable gift. If the IRT is properly worded, the assets owned by the IRT are out of the reach of your creditors and those of your trust beneficiaries—while the assets are in the trust. Below are four examples of IRTs with a summary of the primary purpose of each.

Qualified Personal Residence Trusts

A qualified personal residence trust (QPRT) typically allows you to transfer a home, after the passage of a specified period of time (while you continue to live in and use the home), to one or more family members or other heirs at a value less than the current market value. It involves discounting the value of your gift of the home based on the term (period of time) of the QPRT (e.g., 10 years) using the appropriate government-determined interest rate. This arrangement leads to a reduction in the amount of exemption used or gift tax due for making the gift. If you own a residence in a state that has decoupled from the federal estate tax system, a QPRT may provide the added benefit of eliminating your exposure to any state estate tax that might be due at your death (though, if you are domiciled in a state other than Florida, you may be subject to a current state gift tax in that state when you set the trust up). At the end of the term of the QPRT, the named beneficiaries (i.e., children or a trust for their benefit) will own the home.

Grantor Retained Annuity Trusts

A grantor retained annuity trust (GRAT) is a tax-efficient way to transfer appreciating assets to your heirs, after a stated period of time, while providing several benefits, including the following:

- Allows you to make gifts of property to your children or other heirs (or a trust for their benefit) while retaining an income interest in the property for a period of years;
- Reduces the gift tax value (possibly to zero) of the assets

The Real Florida Natives

At the end of the Great Ice Age, 14,000 years ago, the first Native Americans came into what is now Florida. By the time the Europeans arrived, there were hundreds of different Indian societies throughout the area of "La Florida."

From the Apalachee tribe in the northeastern panhandle to the Matecumbe in the Keys, Florida was the original home of the Tequesta, Calusa, Ocale, Potano, Timucua, Tocobaga, Ais, Jeaga and dozens of other groups. Because of the varied geography, the many Indian cultures adapted to their unusual surroundings.

Surviving and flourishing for thousands of years prior to the European "discovery" of Florida, most of these local Indians were virtually extinct by the middle of the 1800s—primarily as victims of warfare and disease.

Among the best known Indian tribes in Florida today are the Seminole and Miccosukee, many of whom descended from the Creek Indians of Alabama and Georgia. However, there are currently more than 125 other tribes identified in Florida, from Apache to Yurok, with the Cherokee as the largest tribe.

Source: *Florida's Indians from Ancient Times to the Present by Jerald T. Milanich, 1998, University Press of Florida.*

you give to the trust by delaying the actual enjoyment of the property by the beneficiaries for a period of years; and/or

- Removes growth on the assets from your taxable estate, thereby eliminating any gift or estate taxes on the appreciation.

Irrevocable Life Insurance Trusts

The primary purpose of an irrevocable life insurance trust (ILIT) is to own a policy of life insurance outside of your taxable estate, while protecting the cash value and the insurance proceeds from creditors and the IRS. Life insurance is often a very important financial tool in estate tax planning, as it creates needed liquidity for paying taxes and expenses as well as providing tax-free cash for beneficiaries. An ILIT can be designed as a generation-skipping (*dynasty*) trust and can allow the insurance proceeds to benefit more than one generation of family members without the imposition of tax at each generation.

Charitable Remainder Trusts

A charitable remainder trust (CRT) is an irrevocable trust that allows you to make a charitable contribution and diversify your assets without paying immediate income tax, while retaining an income stream. Grantors typically transfer property, usually appreciated stock or appreciated real estate but other assets can also be contributed. The donor of the property typically designates himself or herself as trustee. The donor and spouse generally are the income beneficiaries of the CRT for their lifetimes. This allows the donor beneficiary to retain control of and receive income from the contributed assets. Once transferred into the CRT, the assets are generally free from the claims of creditors. Usually, upon the death of the income beneficiaries, any assets left in the CRT are distributed to one or more charities designated by you, as grantor.

Charitable Remainder Trust Benefits

A charitable remainder trust can accomplish the following:

- Allows you to avoid immediate capital gain tax on the sale of highly appreciated property (e.g., real estate, stocks/bonds);
- Allows you the option to remain in control of the assets contributed because you may be the trustee of your CRT;
- Provides a source of greater income for your life and, possibly, the lives of your spouse and other family members;
- Helps to diversify your assets;
- Provides an income tax deduction and resulting tax savings that may be invested to replace the contribution, possibly through the use of life insurance owned by an ILIT;
- Protects assets from the claims of creditors; and
- Allows you to leave a legacy to your favorite charity or your own foundation at your death.

Asset Protection for Florida Residents

Your decision to become a resident of Florida entitles you to various protections under Florida law. Florida's asset protection laws are among the most liberal, debtor-friendly laws in the country. Florida's favorable asset protection laws cover a Florida resident's personal property and intangible assets, regardless of where the accounts and assets are held. If a Florida resident's real property is located in another state, then the asset protection laws of that state apply to the real property. Here is a summary of many of the protections provided to you when you have declared Florida to be your domicile.

Homestead

As discussed in detail in *Chapter 3: Florida Homestead Exemption*, your Florida homestead—including the full value of your home and up to one-half acre of land in the city limits and

FLORIDA SEA TURTLES

Five species of protected sea turtles are found in Florida waters: the loggerhead, the green, the leatherback, the Kemp's ridley and the hawksbill.

Loggerhead sea turtles are the most common species seen in Florida and the beaches along the Treasure Coast make up the most important loggerhead nesting site in the hemisphere. Females arrive every summer to nest. A female lays around one hundred eggs in a narrow pit she digs, usually in beach sand, with her hind flippers. Once she returns to the ocean, the hatchlings are on their own. If they are lucky, they will reach maturity in twenty-five to thirty-five years and return to the same beach where they were hatched to lay a new generation of eggs.

Reprinted with permission of www.Bigstock.com

Beachfront residents know not to disturb the nests and to turn out their lights at night from May through October to avoid confusing sea turtle hatchlings, which rely on the starlight reflected from the ocean to find their way back to sea.

Source: *www.myfwc.com*

160 contiguous acres outside of a municipality—has constitutional protection from creditors. The protection is subject to provisions of the Bankruptcy Abuse Prevention and Consumer Protection Act of 2005.

Retirement Plans

Florida Statute § 222.21(2)(a) provides that any money or other assets payable to a participant or beneficiary in a qualified retirement plan—including a profit sharing plan, individual retirement account (IRA), Roth IRA, 401(k) plan and other qualified retirement plans—is exempt from all claims of creditors of the beneficiary or participant. However, it is important to note that a recent U.S. Supreme Court decision in Clark v. Rameker concluded that *inherited* IRAs are not afforded the same protection.

In the case of IRAs and Roth IRA accounts, if a bankruptcy is involved, the amount exempted under the 2005 bankruptcy law is limited to $1 million unless the owner can demonstrate that the excess amount represents rollover distributions from one or more qualified retirement plans.

Life Insurance

Under Florida law, the death benefit and cash value of a life insurance policy for owners, insureds and beneficiaries are protected.

Death benefit: Insurance policy proceeds are exempt for any party (owner, insured or beneficiary) if payable to a named beneficiary other than the insured, insured's estate, executors, administrators or assigns.

Cash value: While a Florida resident is alive, the cash surrender value of any insurance policy owned on his/her life or other Florida resident is exempt from the claims of creditors, unless the policy was funded with the intent to defraud creditors.

Annuities

Perhaps the most popular financial product for asset protection planning is an annuity. Florida statutes protect annuities from creditors' claims and Florida courts have liberally construed this statutory exemption to include the broadest range of annuity contracts and arrangements. In fact, Florida protects not only annuities but also annuity payments received by a debtor, so long as they are accurately traceable back to the annuity. Private annuities between family members are entitled to the exemption, as are the proceeds of personal injury settlements structured as an annuity.

Salary or Wages

Florida Statute § 222.11 exempts from creditors an unlimited amount of salary earned from personal labor or services by a debtor who is the *head of household*, if the debtor provides more than fifty percent of the support for a dependent (e.g., a child, spouse or parent). The statute defines head of household as "any natural person who is providing more than one half of the support for a child or other dependent." The wages remain exempt for a period of six months when deposited in a bank account.

Hurricane Saving Accounts

A recent addition to Florida's list of assets protected from creditors is the hurricane savings account. Florida Statute § 222.22 (4)(b) defines a hurricane savings account as an account owned by the owner of homestead property up to twice the amount of an insurance deductible or other uninsurable portion of the risk of loss from a hurricane, windstorm or flood.

College 529 Savings Plans

Named for the section of the Internal Revenue Code that creates and regulates them, 529 plans provide a tax advantaged way for a

Florida's State Pie

The preferred pie of Floridians is the key lime pie. As the official state pie, it beat out its competitors: the pecan pie and sweet potato pie. Key lime pies may have originated with the advent of condensed milk. Without many cows to give milk and no refrigeration, canned milk was popular when it was introduced in the 1850s and locals used it, along with the limes Spanish explorers had brought with them, to make the famous pie.

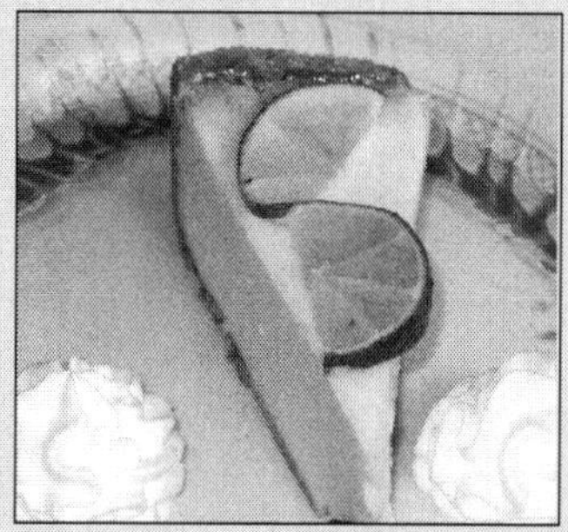

Reprinted with permission of Bigstock.com

Key Lime Pie Recipe

4 large egg yolks
1 (14 oz.) can sweetened condensed milk
1/2 cup key lime juice
Baked 9 inch graham cracker crust
Whipped cream for garnish

*Beat eggs until thick and light yellow. Add sweetened condensed milk. Stir in half of the juice until blended. Add remaining juice and blend in. Pour mixture into graham cracker pie shell (recipe below). Bake at 350°F for 12 to 15 minutes until set. Cool pie and chill in refrigerator. Top with whipped cream before serving.

Graham Cracker Crust

Mix together:
1 1/4 cup graham cracker crumbs
1/4 cup sugar
1/3 cup butter or margarine, melted

*Combine and press into bottom and up sides of a 9" pie pan. Bake in 375°F oven for 6 to 8 minutes until lightly browned. Place on rack to cool. **Note:** It can take up to 12 whole small key limes (6 Persian limes) to make 1/2 cup of the juice. You can use Persian limes or substitute lemon juice for half the amount of juice to get the key lime flavor kick. **Hint:** Peak key lime season is during the summer months. You can juice the limes and freeze them in ice cube trays and then transfer them to sealable plastic bags where they can be stored in your freezer for future pie use.

Source: *from the kitchen of* Florida Domicile Handbook *editor Mollie Page.*

parent or grandparent to invest and save for a descendant's education. Protection of these plans under Florida law depends on where the money is placed. If you invest in a 529 plan located in Florida, the fund is protected under Florida Statute § 222.22 pertaining to prepaid college trust funds.

Disability Income Benefits

Disability income benefits under any disability insurance policy are exempt from legal process in Florida.

Automobile Exemption

Florida residents may protect up to $1,000 of equity in an automobile. The fact that a debtor needs an automobile to go to work does not protect the vehicle from creditors to the extent that the debtor's equity (value less any loan amount) exceeds $1,000.

Miscellaneous Exemptions

Florida statutes include several other narrow asset exemptions, such as professionally prescribed health aids, medical saving accounts and unemployment benefits.

Reasons to Update an Estate Plan

There are many reasons to update your existing estate plan. Among those reasons are:

- **Change in Domicile.** Moving from one state to another may warrant a review of your estate plan to ensure it will work as expected under the laws of the new state (e.g., Florida). For example, if you have an existing revocable living trust and are moving from a state with a state estate and/or state inheritance tax to one without, changing the situs of the trust may be advisable to help prove your intent and avoid claims from your former state of residence.

- **Change in Marital Status.** Separation, marriage and divorce all require major changes to an estate plan. Also, consider prenuptial planning opportunities if marriage is being considered. This could be an especially valuable planning tool when a second marriage is involved.
- **Change in Financial Status.** Winning the lottery will certainly change your financial status but so will selling a business, retiring or receiving an inheritance. Such changes may require adjustments to both your estate and financial plans.
- **Birth or Death.** The birth or adoption of a child or grandchild often leads to the creation of planning vehicles, including various trusts, 529 College Savings Plans, special saving accounts under the Uniform Transfer to Minor's Act (UTMA) or Uniform Gifts to Minor's Act (UGMA)—which is a simple way for a minor to own securities without requiring the services of an attorney to prepare trust documents or the appointment of a trustee, etc. The *death* of a beneficiary may require the addition of new beneficiaries and changes to beneficiary designations. The death of a named trustee or other fiduciary may require adding other names to your existing plan.
- **Changes in Lives of Beneficiaries, Trustees or Fiduciaries.** Common needs for changes include:
    - Marriage, divorce, births or adoptions
    - A beneficiary who has developed a drug habit or become a spendthrift
    - A child or grandchild who has become an adult and, possibly, a good choice to be a successor trustee or other fiduciary

- An existing trustee who has become ill or too old to be named as a successor trustee or other fiduciary
- A former employee or estranged friend named as a beneficiary, trustee or other fiduciary

- **Changes in Estate-planning Law.** Because of the substantial changes brought about by the American Taxpayer Relief Act of 2012 (ATRA), some basic assumptions that shaped most estate plans, especially estate tax thresholds and the new "portability" provision, make revisions almost mandatory. In fact, every estate plan created before 2013 needs to be reviewed and will likely lead to changes and/or additions.

- **Innovation in Estate Planning.** With changes in the law, societal changes and court decisions, estate-planning experts continue to innovate. Many of the new estate planning techniques and strategies could make your existing plan obsolete. This may be reason enough to have your plan reviewed.

- **Asset Protection.** As discussed above, you may become the target of gold-digging plaintiffs. By employing one of the many asset protection strategies, you can reduce your liability exposure and possibly protect yourself and your heirs from exposure to lawsuits.

- **Market Conditions.** Certain market conditions can make certain advanced planning strategies extremely powerful. For example, a low interest rate environment makes the viability of Grantor Retained Annuity Trusts (GRATs), discussed above, and such things as premium financed life insurance attractive planning tools.

QUESTIONS AND ANSWERS

Estate Planning

Q: What is estate planning?

A: Proper estate planning includes living planning, providing for you and your family during life and preparing for the orderly and efficient transfer of your assets at your death. The process of good estate planning involves the preparation of various documents, such as wills, trusts and powers of attorney.

Virtually every plan should start with the goal of allowing you to give what you have to whom you want when you want and in the way you want and, at the same time, paying the least amount of court costs, attorney's fees and estate taxes possible. The process often includes life insurance planning and the use of irrevocable life insurance trusts, revocable living trusts and other ancillary documents, such as living wills and health care surrogate designations or health care powers of attorney.

The "living" part of estate planning includes taking care of your family in the event you become incapacitated during your lifetime; charitable giving strategies that can provide for you and other family members during your life and one or more charities at your death; and retirement planning, gift and income tax planning and protection from creditors.

Q: Does federal or state law govern estate taxes?

A: On the federal level, estate and gift taxes, income tax and generation-skipping transfer tax are governed by the Internal Revenue Code and its regulations and rules. The federal courts settle disputes between taxpayers and the IRS regarding these rules.

Each state, including Florida, has its own statutes with regard to inheritance and gift taxes, as well as wills, trusts, partnerships and so on. Florida courts interpret state statutes in case of disagreements.

Q: Does Florida have a state gift or inheritance tax?

A: Practically speaking, no. Before the enactment of the Economic Growth and Tax Relief Reconciliation Act (EGTRRA) of 2001, Florida, like many states, relied on receiving a portion of the tax charged by the federal estate tax system. This tax was sometimes referred to as a "sponge" or "pickup tax" and often was the only death-related tax charged by the states. However, EGTRRA ended the sharing program, effectively eliminating Florida's estate tax. Many other states have decoupled from the federal system, enacting separate gift, estate and/or inheritance taxes for their residents.

Florida's Constitution mandates full conformity with the federal law under EGTRRA and does not allow the imposition of a decoupled state estate or gift tax. Hence, unless or until there is a change in its constitution, Florida will not have a state gift or estate tax.

Q: Why should I do my estate planning in Florida?

A: Here are some of the many reasons to do your estate planning in Florida:

- Florida has no separate state estate, inheritance or gift tax.
- Florida laws allow you to establish a trust that will last up to 360 years—protecting the assets in trust for your heirs for many generations.
- Florida has no individual income tax, so the earnings on trust assets retained in a Florida irrevocable trust will not be subject to state income tax in Florida.
- As of 2007, Florida has no intangibles tax.
- If any part of your estate is exposed to probate, the probate process in Florida is relatively simple and can be completed in a timely fashion.
- Another benefit is the significant number of Florida-based attorneys, CPAs, trust officers, financial planners and insurance professionals who specialize in estate planning.

How to Choose a Charity

Donating to a charity not only helps others but you as well. As a donor, you can benefit economically, psychologically, spiritually and socially. But how do you know which charity is right for you? These three questions can help you start the process and find a charity that's worthy of your money.

1. What matters most to you?
Before you open your checkbook or name a benefactor, make sure to clarify your beliefs and preferences. Do they align with the leadership of the charity? Are you comfortable giving to a small, community charity or would you prefer to give to a national organization? What causes do you hold dear to your heart? Education? Animals? The environment?

2. Is the charity legitimate?
Don't get caught in a scam. Read up on the organization outside of its website before deciding to make a donation. Legitimate charities should have bylaws and must file taxes. It's also advisable to ask to see the charity's annual report or a copy of its latest financial audit.

Beyond being legitimate, you want to make sure the charity is reaching its goal(s) and/or being ethical. Talk to its clients and find out how significant the charity's work is in their daily lives. Is the charity making a measurable impact in the community?

3. Does it feel right?
It's okay to not pick the most popular charity or one that comes highly recommended. If you feel uncomfortable or have doubts, keep researching until you feel confident your donation can help a worthy organization. Trust your instincts.

Source: *http://www.guidestar.org*

Q. I have recently done my estate planning in my previous state. Why should I redo my planning in Florida?

A. Estate and probate laws vary from state to state. Consequently, if you are relocating to Florida, you should review the peculiarities of Florida law with a qualified Florida estate-planning attorney to determine the appropriateness and effectiveness of your current estate plan. Although you may not need to rewrite your entire estate plan, there may be good reasons for considering some revisions or additions. In addition, to help establish your intent to be domiciled in Florida, your estate-planning documents should reflect that you are now a Florida resident.

Q: Is my out-of-state will effective in Florida?

A: Most states, including Florida, recognize an out-of-state will as valid as long as it is written and executed according to the requirements of the state in which you were domiciled when it was signed. However, while validly executed out-of-state wills remain effective in Florida, the provisions of such wills may be interpreted under Florida law and, thus, the results in Florida may be different than in other states. Also, to help establish your intent to be domiciled in Florida, your will should be revised to recite that you are a Florida resident.

Q: If I change my domicile to Florida, will I owe any tax in my former state of residence at my death?

A: Your estate may be subject to death taxation in another state if you own real property or certain other tangible assets in that state and/or if that state successfully claims that you were domiciled there at the time of your death. Depending on the laws of that state and the type of estate tax imposed, there are additional steps that you may take as a Florida resident to minimize the impact of any such tax.

Q: Now that I am becoming a Florida resident, should I change my personal representative in my out-of-state planning documents?

A: If your will names a nonresident individual as personal

representative, he or she will not be allowed to qualify in Florida unless related to you in the manner provided by Florida statute.

If your will names an out-of-state trust company or bank as your personal representative or trustee, you should confirm that the trust company or bank will qualify to exercise fiduciary powers in Florida. If you have a trust that names an individual residing far from Florida as trustee, it may not be practical to expect such an individual to carry out his or her responsibilities.

Q: Are provisions of my will subject to different legal interpretations under Florida Law?

A: Laws governing the interpretation of wills vary from state to state. Your will should be reviewed by a Florida attorney to determine whether Florida law may defeat your estate planning goals. For example, if you have a provision attempting to pass your Florida homestead property to someone in violation of Florida law, the provision would be unenforceable in Florida.

Q: What effect does Florida law have on me if my spouse and I have moved to Florida from a community property state?

A. Community property affects the rights of you and your spouse in determining certain income and estate tax liabilities, as well as property rights under Florida law. If you are relocating to Florida from a community property state, you should meet with an estate-planning professional to review your estate plan to avoid unanticipated and undesirable tax consequences. For example, community property is entitled to federal income tax benefits that can be preserved even after you become domiciled in Florida.

Q: After relocating to Florida, when do estate-planning documents need to be reviewed?

A: Virtually all estate plans should be reviewed when there has been one or more changes in your life, such as a birth, death, remarriage, change in your financial picture or move to another state (i.e., Florida). You should also consider meeting with your Florida attorney or financial planner when there has been a change

Florida's Economic Strengths

According to the U.S. Department of Commerce, Florida's GDP (gross domestic product) is predicted to increase, on average, 4 percent a year. Data shows Florida has recovered or replaced almost two-thirds of the jobs it lost during the recession.

International trade: The state produced and exported goods worth over $64 billion in 2016 and the two years prior.

Tourism: Out-of-state visitor spending reached $108 billion in 2015. These out-of-state visitors spent an average of $300 million per day, indirectly supporting 1.4 million jobs.

Space industry: Florida is home to over 2,000 aerospace and aviation companies employing over 87,000 workers. The space industry contributes billions to the state's economy.

Agriculture: Florida is second only to Brazil in global orange juice production. More than 70 percent of America's citrus industry is located in Florida. This $9 billion industry employs more than 75,000 Floridians.

Construction: This industry's strength results from the steady stream of new residents to Florida each year. Construction is the fastest growing industry in Florida, growing at 5.9% annually.

University research: More than 700,000 Florida jobs are attributed to the State University System.

Sources: *Florida Dept. of State; Visit Florida, Flblog.edu/pressroom/did-u-know.php; U.S. Census Bureau; State University System of Florida/Board of Governors, The Bureau of Economic & Business Research (University of Florida) and The Florida Chamber of Commerce.*

in the tax laws. Beyond that, it makes good sense to review your estate plan documents with your attorney every two or three years to be sure they still meet your estate planning goals and to take advantage of any new planning strategies.

Q: What is the biggest problem in estate planning?

A: The biggest problem in estate planning is procrastination. It is human nature to put off things that seem unpleasant but ignoring estate planning may hurt those you love most. And with proper planning, you can realize many living benefits.

Over 55 percent of those who died last year in the United States did so without a will or any planning whatsoever. Many of those people would turn over in their graves if they knew what happened to the assets they left behind.

If you die without an estate plan, you die intestate, allowing the state to dictate how your assets will pass among your heirs. The state's plan often does not come close to matching what you would really want to happen. In Florida, if you are married, only half of your estate assets will pass to your spouse if you have children; the other half will pass to your children, immediately and outright. This distribution could have a dramatic and undesirable effect on the family.

Q: Should my children be part of the estate planning process?

A: While it may feel uncomfortable to discuss estate planning matters with children, it often makes good sense to do so. Giving adult children a summary view of your estate plan can help avoid unnecessary problems or misunderstandings that can occur after you are dead.

When people die, it is not unusual for family members to get into disputes because a parent's intentions were never clarified. Even if you don't discuss specific amounts with your children, you should consider discussing the structure of your estate plan.

Q: What is the role of the probate court?

A: A probate court is the forum in which legal proceedings occur if you are no longer able to manage your affairs because of your incapacity, mental disability or death.

In the case of death, the probate court process transfers ownership of assets titled in your individual name to your heirs. In effect, probate is the process of proving the validity of your will. This process can take weeks, months or even years to complete, depending upon the size, complexity and design of your estate plan. With proper planning (i.e., through the use of a fully funded revocable living trust), it is possible to completely avoid, where desirable, the probate process and the court administration that follows the proving of the will.

The probate process in Florida is relatively simple and is normally completed in a reasonable period of time; however, there are other aspects to consider, such as the cost of probate and the public nature of probate proceedings.

In the event you become incapacitated, you and your family must contend with the guardianship process, which is, in essence, a living probate. Guardianship is designed to protect you and your assets while you are incapable of doing so yourself. Guardianship can be an expensive and time-consuming process.

Like the probate process, guardianship can often be avoided completely with a properly funded revocable living trust.

Q: I have a will. Doesn't that mean my heirs will avoid probate?

A: No. It is a mistake to assume that by having a will you have eliminated probate. Just the opposite is true; unless your assets are titled in a manner that avoids probate, a will very nearly guarantees probate because only a court can prove the validity of a will.

Q: What is so bad about probate?

A: There are numerous reasons why it is best to avoid probate, even in Florida where the probate process is considered simpler than in many other states. Some of those reasons include:

Cost: In many states, the cost associated with probating your estate, including personal representative fees, attorney fees, probate costs and so on, often exceeds 6 percent of the value of the estate. In Florida, your family may experience real savings in legal fees if you incorporate a properly funded RLT into your estate plan.

Time delay: Probate takes time and in many states, including Florida, probate can easily take a year or more before the estate is fully settled. Depending upon the size of your estate or the nature of your assets, you can save your family excessive time delays if you minimize or eliminate your exposure to probate.

Complexity: If you have property, such as real estate, in more than one state, your heirs will likely face separate probate proceedings in each state where the property is located. These multiple probates, called ancillary administration, can significantly add to the cost and time delay of settling an estate.

Public exposure: Although your financial information may not be available to the public, the terms of your will may very well be open to public inspection.

Contests: The public nature of the court process may make it easier for unwanted third parties, such as disgruntled family members, ex-spouses, in-laws and creditors, to contest the estate.

Q: What is the best way to avoid probate?

A: Assets held in an RLT are not subject to the probate process. Although there are limitations to any trust arrangement, if your objective is to avoid the cost, time delays, publicity and complexity inherent in the probate process, an RLT is often the best method to accomplish this. Certain assets, such as a bank account or brokerage account, may pass by designation (called a transfer or pay-on-death designation). Although such a designation may avoid a probate, the asset with such a designation could still get caught up in the guardianship process if you become incapacitated.

Q: Why not put everything in joint tenancy to avoid probate?

A: Joint tenancy with the right of survivorship (or tenancy by the entirety between spouses) is one of the most common and simplest forms of estate planning. When the first of the joint tenants dies, the jointly owned assets pass, by law, to the other tenant, completely avoiding probate. If the remaining joint tenant is a spouse, no estate tax would normally be due. However, there are hidden risks associated with this planning strategy.

Each joint tenant can be held responsible for actions of the other tenant. For example, titling an automobile jointly with a spouse or child who later becomes involved in an accident can cause you to be named as a defendant in a lawsuit resulting from that accident.

You could lose control of bank accounts, stock accounts, annuities, mutual funds and so forth, because either joint tenant may be able to sell such assets without the permission or knowledge of the other owner.

If one joint owner has a problem with a creditor or judgment in a lawsuit, the other owner could lose the asset through court action or garnishment. Although this problem may be avoided with a special form of joint tenancy between spouses, known as tenancy by the entirety, protection could be lost if one spouse dies. For example, assume a married couple owns an asset as tenants by the entirety and the husband has a judgment against him (but not his wife). In this case, the asset is protected from the husband's creditor. However, if the wife predeceases the husband, the protection is lost.

Some jointly held property cannot be sold if one of the joint owners either cannot, because of illness, or will not sign.

Joint tenancy can also result in unintended disinheritance. For example, Jason and Amy both have a child and grandchildren from previous marriages. If Jason dies first and their property is held jointly, Amy can disinherit Jason's child and grandchildren by leaving the assets only to her child and grandchildren.

There may be gift tax implications. For example, Louise purchased a Florida condominium and titled it in her name and her stepdaughter's name as joint owners. By doing so, Louise may have made a gift to her stepdaughter equal to 50 percent of the value of the home. Louise exposed herself to a substantial federal gift tax on the amounts above any unused exemption.

Joint owners receive the assets all at once, even when they may not be able to manage them. Also, if the joint tenants die in a common accident, each tenant, depending upon state law, is entitled to one-half of the assets, which would then cause two probate proceedings.

Q: Is probate ever desirable?

A. Florida probate laws are designed to settle creditors' claims quickly upon a decedent's death (e.g., possibly as short as three months). In the absence of a probate proceeding, creditors' claims may not be completely settled for two years after a decedent's death. As a result, when there is concern about the deceased person's liabilities, a probate proceeding is desirable.

Q: What is the purpose of a will?

A: A will allows you to direct who receives your assets at the time of your death. Without a will, you will die intestate. As a Florida resident, Florida will determine the distribution of your assets in accordance with Florida's intestacy laws.

Your will is revocable during your lifetime. It does not avoid probate. It directs the probate court regarding your wishes. Your will does not control property that you hold as a joint tenant. Also, life insurance, annuities, IRAs and qualified plan assets pass to your heirs—by a separate document known as a beneficiary designation—outside of the will unless you have named your estate as your beneficiary in that document.

Wills can create trusts at your death, known as testamentary trusts, or a will can direct that specific assets be distributed (or poured-over) to a preexisting trust at your death. Wills cannot, however, provide for your care in the event you become incapacitated or disabled.

Q: What is a revocable living trust?

A: A revocable living trust (RLT) is a legal document typically drafted by an attorney. It acts like a will in that it contains your directions for the management and distribution of your assets upon your death. Unlike a will, however, an RLT also contains your instructions for the management of your assets in the event of your disability.

You are the grantor (or trust maker) of the trust agreement and you and possibly your spouse, if named, are beneficiaries of the trust during your lifetime. In most situations, you would name yourself and possibly your spouse as trustees. Thus, you continue to control and manage your assets like you did before you set up the RLT.

To avoid probate, you need to fund your trust by transferring or retitling your assets from your name to yourself (or whomever else you designate) as trustee of your trust. As trustee of your own RLT, you maintain full control over trust property during your lifetime. You also continue to file your income tax returns as you have in the past (using your social security number) and can buy, sell or give away trust property. With this control, you can change, alter or revoke the terms of the trust any time you wish.

At your death, the trust may terminate or, depending upon your instructions, continue for the benefit of your family and other heirs. Much like a will, your RLT contains instructions on how you want the trust assets distributed (e.g., outright or to continue in trust) to your beneficiaries at your death. A Florida trust can be designed to split into two or more trusts (e.g., one for each beneficiary) and continue for up to 360 years.

Q: How does an RLT avoid probate?

A: When an RLT is properly funded with all your pertinent assets, there is no need to probate the trust assets as the RLT is still alive; that is, it is considered a living entity. This is true whether you are incapacitated or deceased. The RLT merely continues in accordance with the terms of your trust.

Q: Why do I need an RLT if I become disabled?

A: Without an RLT that provides for your care during any disability, your loved ones may have to take you through the legal process of what is known as a living probate, or guardianship, with the help of attorneys and a probate judge. Even though your spouse or adult children would most likely be appointed by the court to manage your affairs, they would have to report annually to the court and would be subject to all the legal costs and red tape of the court system. This cumbersome and often needlessly bureaucratic court process would likely continue for as long as you are disabled.

An RLT allows you to choose, in detail, how you want your affairs handled and permits you to set the priorities that you want followed. Furthermore, your successor trustees will be able to manage your financial and other affairs beginning almost immediately when you are incapacitated, without the intervention and potential delays of any court.

Q. Do I need an RLT if I have a durable power of attorney?

A. Yes. Even though a durable power of attorney is designed to be effective if you become incapacitated, the power of attorney may be of no use if a court declares you incompetent and imposes a guardianship (despite your attempt to avoid guardianship) or a financial institution declines to honor the document.

Q. Can't I simply leave my assets to my loved ones? Why should I consider a trust?

A. Generally speaking, it is not a good idea to leave anything of any consequence to your loved ones outright or free of trust. By leaving everything in trust for your heirs' benefit, you can protect them in ways they cannot achieve for themselves.

For example, you could specify in your trust that each of your children is to serve as the trustee of his or her own separate trust, alone or along with one or more co-trustees for his or her lifetime, and that each child's trust provides for their needs as they arise. It would allow each child to manage his or her own funds in the way he or she desires; yet, by retaining everything in trust, you have, to some degree, protected each child's assets from the claims of creditors, which could arise from a failed business venture, an accident or even a spouse in a divorce.

By leaving assets in trust, you may be concerned that your children will think you are controlling them from the grave. However, with the assistance of a qualified attorney, you may be able to provide a great deal of latitude to your children without jeopardizing the benefits of a trust. A qualified attorney can draft your trust in accordance with your wishes, with terms that are as restrictive or liberal as you choose.

Q: Do I need a will if I have an RLT?

A: Yes. A revocable living trust is very powerful and, effectively, acts as your will. However, because some people fail to transfer all their assets into (or fully fund) their RLT, you should also execute a pour-over will, which acts as a safety net and instructs your executor or personal representative to place those assets in your RLT, after going through probate, so that they can be managed and distributed according to the instructions in your trust.

To avoid subjecting any portion of your estate to probate, you should periodically review how your assets are titled to make sure all appropriate assets are titled in your name, as trustee of your trust. Note that some assets should not be titled in your RLT, such as annuities and retirement plan assets.

Annuities and retirement plan assets, including IRAs, can pass at your death by a beneficiary designation form if you complete one before your death. Another asset that you should seriously consider leaving outside your RLT is your Florida homestead.

Your Florida homestead, aside from being one of your most valuable assets, is given a great deal of protection from creditors. However, a question arose several years ago in federal bankruptcy court as to whether a Florida homestead loses its creditor protection if it is owned in an RLT. Although many believe Florida law is quite clear that the Florida homestead would still be protected if owned by an RLT, the uncertainty caused by the federal bankruptcy court suggests that you may want to own your home outside an RLT.

Q: If I have an RLT, will it help my family avoid paying estate taxes?

A: A properly funded RLT avoids probate at your death. However, probate and the federal estate tax have nothing to do with each other. To save federal estate taxes, your attorney could incorporate certain estate tax planning provisions into your RLT.

Q: Does an RLT protect me from creditors?

A: No. As trustee of your RLT, you have the ability to control the assets in your trust and, as the trust maker, you have the ability to revoke the trust at any time. Thus, the assets in an RLT are at the same risk in the event of a judgment against you as they would be if they were titled directly in your name. However, it is possible to design your trust to protect your assets from your beneficiaries' creditors—including spouses in a divorce situation—after your death.

Umbrella insurance policies are inexpensive and cover a wide variety of risks and perils. Any person with assets worth protecting should consider purchasing an umbrella insurance policy.

Q: Who should be my trustee after I die or become disabled?

A: You can name more than one trustee but whomever you select should be someone you trust. Your successor trustee should be a person (or persons) or institution that you have confidence in and that has the ability to handle financial matters. In addition, the trustee you select should be familiar with your objectives and should carry out distributions according to the guidelines you have established in your RLT and overall estate plan.

You should also make sure that the person or institution will accept the responsibilities of acting as your trustee. Furthermore, it is always wise to name alternate trustees in case your initial choices should later be unable or unwilling to serve as trustee.

Q: What is so important about funding an RLT?

A: One of the biggest mistakes in estate planning is failing to fund or transfer ownership of your assets to yourself, as trustee of your RLT. By failing to fund your RLT, you have guaranteed that those assets not titled in the trust will end up going through probate—which is the very thing you were trying to avoid and one of the primary reasons for setting up the trust.

Q: How do I fund my RLT?

A: Funding your trust is not difficult and your financial advisors can likely help you. For example, your estate-planning attorney can help prepare the appropriate deeds to transfer real estate and your attorney, financial advisor, CPA or banker can help you transfer other financial assets, such as investment and bank accounts, to your RLT.

Q: When I retitle my assets, will I need to give a copy of my RLT to the various financial institutions?

A: Not necessarily. To protect themselves from potential legal liability, your investment brokerage firm and bank will need to know who has authority to act on your behalf. Thus, it is likely they will ask for a copy of the trust. However, it is usually sufficient to supply them with a portion of your RLT, such as the cover page, signature page and the section listing your authority, as trustee, over the trust assets. Alternatively, many estate-planning attorneys provide a short document—sometimes known as a memorandum of trust or affidavit of trust—that should suffice.

Q: Since my RLT acts as my will, what type of information should the trust include?

A: Just as in the preparation of your will, you should consider the following questions:

- Who do you want to inherit your assets and in what amounts or percentages?

- How do you want to time the distributions of your assets to your various heirs?
- Who would you like to receive specific assets, such as your personal effects (e.g., car, watch, jewelry and artwork)?
- Should you leave assets outright or, as suggested above, in one or more trusts?
- If you decide on leaving assets in trust, who should act as the trustee of each trust?
- Does it make sense to have a co-trustee, such as a trust company, attorney or CPA, for certain trusts for a period of time or for the life of the trust?

Q: Am I required by Florida law to leave a certain portion of my estate to my surviving spouse?

A: Under the laws of Florida, your surviving spouse may elect to receive 30 percent of your estate (plus the value of certain lifetime transfers) at your death, even if such a gift were against your wishes. This right is called the elective share. You should consult with an attorney to ensure that your estate plan properly considers the elective share.

Lovebug Season

Harmless to humans, lovebug season occurs twice a year, May and September, and lasts about four weeks. This is when the bugs mate and can be seen attached to one another. They are usually active between the hours of 10 a.m. and 6 p.m. in temperatures above 84 degrees. Lovebugs congregate near highways because they are attracted to decomposing plant debris but often confuse the odor with chemicals from exhaust fumes.

Source: *http://solutionsforyourlife.ufl.edu/hot_topics/environment/lovebugs.html*

For example, your estate plan may be designed to hold your spouse's elective share in trust (rather than distributing it outright to your spouse). Note that a spouse's right to an elective share at your death may be restricted or eliminated with a pre- or post-marital agreement.

Q: Is it possible to distribute a portion of my estate to my children and other heirs upon my death and the remainder of my assets to them upon my spouse's death?

A: Yes. However, it is important to consider the tax ramifications of making distributions to anyone other than your spouse. There is an unlimited marital deduction on gifts to your spouse during your lifetime and at your death. If distributions to your heirs, other than your spouse, do not exceed your remaining applicable federal estate exemption at your death, no federal estate tax would be due. However, if you are not domiciled in Florida, your state of residence may have a state estate and/or inheritance tax and an exemption below the current federal estate tax exemption, thereby exposing your estate to state taxes. If you are domiciled in Florida and own real estate in another state with an estate tax, your estate may have to pay tax if the value of the real estate is above that state's specific exemption.

Note that you should always consult an estate-planning attorney when designing your estate plan. This is especially true if your spouse is not a U.S. citizen as the tax laws are different.

Tax issues aside, you are generally free to distribute your property at death any way you wish, subject to your surviving spouse's rights, as discussed above, and claims by your creditors.

Q: What will happen if I become incapacitated?

A: Many people fail to address the question of incapacity (incompetency) before it becomes a serious issue. By not acting, you may unnecessarily subject your family to the probate court and all its administrative bureaucracy. Failing to provide for someone to look after you in the event of your incapacity will cause the court to appoint a guardian for you. These individuals or institutions may or may not be the persons or organizations you would choose if you were able to do so. And even if they were, you would likely incur the expenses and delays of the judicial process.

To avoid what could become a bureaucratic nightmare, your RLT should appoint one or more successor trustees who will take over for you during your period of disability. In addition, in a separate document known as a durable power of attorney, you should authorize one or more individuals to transfer property that is not in your RLT specifically to your RLT so that your trustee can use it to care for you during your disability under the terms of your trust.

Q: How do I arrange for someone to have authority to make health care decisions for me in the event I am unable to do so?

A: Florida law allows you to designate a health care surrogate to make health care decisions, including whether to remove life support, in the event you are unable to make such decisions yourself.

Q: Should I provide for how I want my personal property distributed?

A: Yes. Your RLT can include provisions allowing you to make up a written instrument, often referred to as a memorandum of tangible personal property, to control the manner in which you want your personal effects distributed. You should keep this document with your RLT documentation.

Q: I am considering retiring in Florida but want to be certain my dog is cared for when I am gone. Does Florida allow pets to inherit assets?

A: Yes. Florida is a pet-friendly state and allows the creation of a trust to provide for the care and well-being of an animal. Speak to your Florida attorney about including provisions to benefit your dog and other pets in your estate-planning papers.

" I've invested my heart and soul in this company.
I need a receipt for tax purposes. "

I am a great believer in luck.
The harder I work, the more of it I seem to have.
–Coleman Cox

CHAPTER 5

DOING BUSINESS IN FLORIDA

Florida is known for its warm weather, beautiful beaches and numerous golf courses but it is also a business owner's paradise. The World Bank forecasts that by 2019, Florida's economy will be the 16th largest economy in the world! Given our country's aging baby boomer generation and their continuing migration to warmer climates, business opportunities in Florida are expected to grow. With a huge market, business-friendly legislature, competitive cost of doing business, well-educated and well-trained workforce and highly attractive lifestyle, many companies around the country and world are taking a serious look at relocating to Florida.

For those business owners who cannot move their business operations to Florida, other tax-efficient planning strategies may be available when the owner becomes domiciled in Florida. Many business owners have been able to restructure their company's management, in whole or at least in part, so they can manage the business from Florida. Often, business owners who spend a lot of time in Florida are already making daily phone calls, reviewing reports, managing cash and receivables, monitoring liabilities, responding to email and voicemail, contacting clients/prospects remotely and conducting conference calls from Florida.

These business owners can create a consulting company in Florida and receive consulting fees for services benefiting their northern business while they reside in Florida, thereby converting the income derived from the consulting business into Florida income and avoiding state income tax in their northern state. Of course, Florida income is not subject to state income tax in the Sunshine State and business owners can enjoy substantial savings from restructuring an out-of-state business in this way.

Florida Business Taxes

Most businesses are subject to sales and use taxes and, in some counties, a discretionary add-on sales tax. Businesses are also subject to unemployment taxes and intangible personal property taxes. Depending on the entity type, state corporate income taxes may be levied as well.

Most Florida businesses must also collect and submit sales taxes and must, therefore, register as a sales and use tax dealer before conducting business.

While a detailed discussion of the possible taxes affecting a Florida business goes beyond the scope of this book, there are four taxes (sales and use tax, discretionary sales surtax, unemployment tax and corporate income tax) worth emphasizing, since many businesses are subject to them.

Sales and Use Tax

Sales tax applies to the sale, rental, lease or license to use goods, certain services and commercial property in Florida, unless the transaction is specifically exempt. If your business involves taxable transactions, you must register as a sales and use tax dealer before you begin conducting business in Florida. Currently, the sales tax in Florida is set at six percent.

Dealers are responsible for collecting sales tax at the time of each sale and for remitting the tax for each collection period to the Department of Revenue (DOR), along with a Sales and Use Tax Return (Form DR-15). Any use tax due must also be accrued and remitted on your tax return. You must file even if no tax is due. If the opening date of your business is delayed, you must notify the DOR to avoid a notice of delinquency and a late-filing penalty.

Discretionary Sales Surtax for Businesses

As discussed previously for individuals, Florida counties are authorized to levy a discretionary sales surtax on most business transactions that occur in a county that has adopted the discretionary surtax.

A dealer who sells and delivers taxable merchandise or a taxable service to a location within a county imposing a discretionary surtax must collect the surtax at the rate imposed in the county where the merchandise or service is delivered. The surtax is levied on the first $5,000 of any item of tangible personal property. The $5,000 limit does not apply to commercial rentals, transient rentals or services.

Dealers remit discretionary sales surtax to the Florida Department of Revenue, along with sales and use tax, on the Sales and Use Tax Return (Form DR-15).

Unemployment Tax

Unemployment compensation provides partial, temporary income to workers who lose their jobs through no fault of their own and who remain able and available for work. The employer pays for unemployment compensation through a tax administered by the Department of Revenue.

Workers do not pay any part of the unemployment tax and employers must not make payroll deductions for this purpose. The employer's payments go into a reserve fund from which benefits are paid to eligible claimants. After a qualifying period, employers with a stable employment history will receive credit for this in a reduced tax rate.

Employers are required to file an Employer's Quarterly Report (Form UCT-6) each quarter, regardless of employment activity or whether any taxes are due.

Corporate Income Tax

S Corporations, partnerships, limited liability companies taxed as partnerships and tax-exempt organizations are generally not required to file a Florida corporate income tax return. However, entities that pay federal income tax itself, rather than passing the liability through to its owners, may be required to file a Florida corporate income tax return and pay any tax due.

GEOGRAPHY: SOUTH FLORIDA

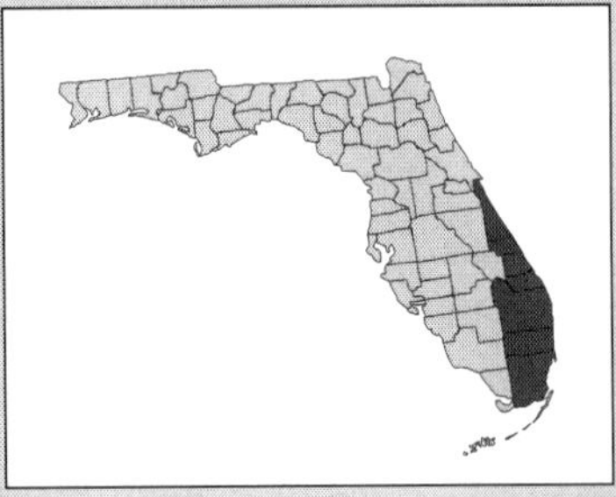

South Florida refers primarily to Florida's southeast coast, from Fort Pierce south to Key West. The major cities in South Florida are Miami, Fort Lauderdale and West Palm Beach. Visitors flock to Miami Beach for its Latin vibe and wild nightlife. Miami is also home to the Miami Dolphins, the Marlins, the Miami Heat, Miami Seaquarium, Fairchild Tropical Gardens and countless shopping opportunities. Just north, Palm Beach County offers some of the best golfing in Florida and Everglades National Park is a short drive west with wildlife viewing, airboat tours, canoeing and camping.

Facts About South Florida

Miami Beach pharmacist Benjamin Green invented the first suntan cream in 1944. He accomplished this development by cooking cocoa butter in a granite coffee pot on his wife's stove.

Key West has the highest average temperature in the United States—at just above 78 degrees Fahrenheit.

Miami installed the first automated bank teller machine especially for inline skaters.

The Morikami Museum and Japanese Gardens, on 200 acres in Delray Beach, is the only museum in the United States dedicated exclusively to the living culture of Japan.

Fort Lauderdale is known as the Venice of America because the city has 185 miles of local waterways.

Islamorada is billed as the Sports Fishing Capital of the World. Key Largo is known as the Diving Capital of the World.

Fort Zachary Taylor in Key West was built between 1845 and 1866. Controlled by the Union during the Civil War, the fort was the home base for a successful blockade of Confederate ships that some historians say shortened the conflict by a full year. The fort also was active during the Spanish-American War, World War I and World War II.

The Florida Museum of Hispanic and Latin American Art in Coral Gables is the first and only museum in the United States dedicated to the preservation, diffusion and promotion of Hispanic and Latin American Art.

Source: *www.50states.com/facts/florida.htm.*

C Corporations that conduct business or earn or receive income in Florida must file a Florida corporate income tax return unless specifically exempted by law. The return must be filed even if no tax is due. The corporate income tax rate is 5.5 percent of net income. A 3.3 percent alternative minimum tax may apply if it results in more income tax payable than the corporate income tax rate of 5.5 percent.

QUESTIONS AND ANSWERS

Florida Business

Q: How do I register my business to collect and submit sales taxes in Florida?

A: Businesses may register online at the Florida Department of Revenue's website or complete a paper application to collect and report tax in Florida (Form DR-1).

Q: Does the state of Florida publish any resources on starting or moving a business to Florida?

A: Yes. New business registrants can find many downloadable and printable resources by visiting floridarevenue.com and searching "Start-up Kit for New Business Owners."

Q: How can I learn more about Florida's business-related taxes?

A: You can find additional information about Florida's business-related taxes at www.floridarevenue.com or by calling (800) 352-3671 (Florida only).

REST IN PEACE

Because of its asset protection laws, Florida is home to many stars. It is also the final resting place of these famous stars:

Ronnie Van Zant: Lead singer of the popular rock band, Lynyrd Skynyrd, was born and buried in Jacksonville.

Bo Diddley: This influential musician and rock and roll legend is buried in Bronson.

The Ashley Gang: One of Florida's most notorious gang of bank robbers are ironically buried in Stuart, a residential area full of bankers and millionaires.

Perry Como: Legendary crooner, Como had 14 singles that made it to No. 1 and sold more than 100 million albums. In 1958, he won a Grammy Award as best male singer for the hit "Catch a Falling Star." He is buried in Palm Beach County.

Gene Sarazen: This professional golfer, known for his double-eagle in the 1935 Masters and for being the first golfer to win all four major championships, is buried in Marco Island.

Edgar J. Watson: Better known as E.J. Watson, the notorious, alleged Everglades mass murderer (also accused of killing Belle Starr) is buried in Fort Myers.

Francis X. Endres: A man who brought animation to life with his creations of Popeye, Betty Boop, Felix the Cat and Superman. Endres is buried in Fort Lauderdale.

Rocky Marciano: Heavyweight Champion of the World from 1952 to 1956, Rocky is buried in Fort Lauderdale.

Source: *Floridafringetourism.com*

"I'd like you to meet my children, Occupant and Resident."

PART 2

HOW TO ESTABLISH FLORIDA DOMICILE

Your *domicile* and your *residence* are not necessarily the same thing. You may have more than one residence in more than one state but, for tax purposes, you may claim only one domicile. The term "domicile" represents a subjective concept and principally refers to *a matter of intent*. In other words, it is where you intend to have your home base; it is your true, fixed and permanent state of residence. However, if you do not properly establish a clear intent to change your domicile to Florida, it is possible that your former state of domicile may claim you as a resident of that state and tax you accordingly.

Proving your intent is important for two primary reasons. The first is to eliminate or reduce your exposure to income taxes from your former state and, second, to avoid any state estate and/or state inheritance taxes upon your death.

Your legal domicile at your death can have a significant impact on the taxation of your estate. While nearly all states claim that a person can have only one domicile, each state has the right to apply its own definition of the term. To complicate matters, federal tax law does not alleviate the problem with a definition of its own. For example, when Howard Hughes died, multiple states wanted to tax his estate. The U.S. Supreme Court refused to settle the dispute, ruling that each state had the authority to impose its estate tax on residents who they believed were domiciled in their state at death.

In another famous case, the states of Florida, Texas, New York and Massachusetts each claimed Colonel Edward H. R. Green, son of the legendary Hetty Green, was domiciled in their state at the time of his death, saying they were entitled to collect death taxes on his tangible property within their respective states and on his intangible property wherever located. None of the states reduced its tax claim to a judgment but all conceded that the decedent's estate was insufficient to satisfy the total amount of taxes claimed.

Similarly, in the case of Hill vs. Martin, the U. S. Supreme Court allowed Pennsylvania and New Jersey both to claim domicile and tax the estate of Dr. John Thompson Dorrance, the founder of the Campbell Soup Company. As a result, each state collected approximately $17 million in state estate taxes from his estate.

It is important to note that, for purposes of estate tax, real or tangible property (i.e., real estate, automobiles, jewelry, etc.) may be subject to tax in the state *where the property is located*, regardless of your legal domicile. However, intangible property (i.e., stocks, bonds, notes, bank accounts, etc.) will generally be taxed only in the state of your domicile. Since Florida does not currently have an estate or gift tax, no state tax would be due on intangible assets or on tangible assets located in Florida that are gifted or bequeathed to others—when Florida domicile has been properly established. Thus, if you have real or personal property in multiple states, depending upon the location of those assets at the time of your death, there may be some tax due in the states where those assets are located. If an asset cannot be moved (i.e., real estate) during your lifetime, depending upon state law where the asset is located, it may be possible to avoid exposure to state estate taxes by placing the asset in a Family Limited Liability Company or Family Limited Partnership (see Chapter 4 for more details), thereby converting your property to an intangible asset.

Clearly establishing Florida as your state of domicile can help you avoid the unnecessary imposition of income taxes and any state estate and/or inheritance taxes from other states. Through careful planning, as discussed in the next chapter, you can firmly establish your intention to domicile in Florida and avoid exposure to multiple taxation as well as the expense and stress of having to defend yourself in a challenge from your former state of residence.

Spring or Spa?

Once prescribed by holistic doctors, swimming in a natural spring provides immeasurable joy for tourists and Floridians. Here are a few spring destinations that won't disappoint:

Blue Spring – Orange City, FL
De Leon Springs State Park – De Leon Springs, FL
Edward Ball Wakulla Springs State Park – Wakulla Springs, FL
Ellie Schiller Homosassa Springs Wildlife State Park – Homosassa, FL
Fanning Springs State Park – Fanning Springs, FL
Ichetucknee Springs State Park – Fort White, FL
Manatee Springs State Park – Chiefland, FL
Peacock Springs State Park – Live Oak, FL
Ponce De Leon Springs State Park – Ponce De Leon, FL
Rainbow Springs State Park – Dunnellon, FL
Weeki Wachee Springs State Park – Spring Hill, FL
Wekiwa Springs State Park – Apopka, FL

Source: *Floridastateparks.org*

ACTION STEPS TO PROVE YOUR INTENT

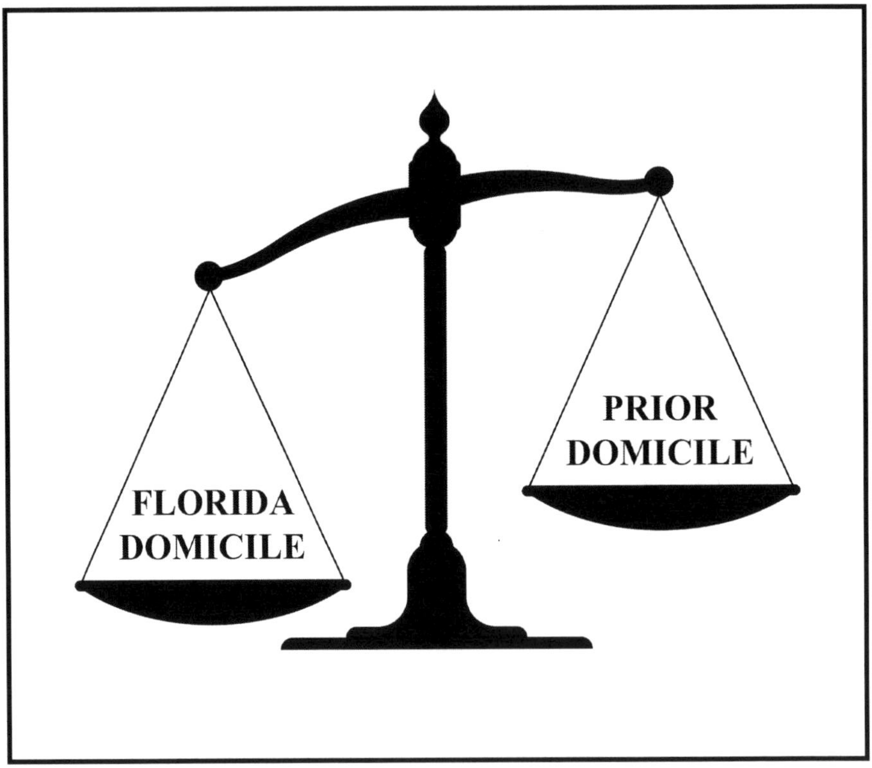

The bad news is time flies.
The good news is you're the pilot.
–Michael Altshuler

CHAPTER 6

CHANGING YOUR DOMICILE: A STEP-BY-STEP GUIDE

To become domiciled in Florida, you must subjectively intend to become domiciled in Florida. Because it is impossible to conclusively determine a person's subjective intent, courts that have been called upon to determine a person's true intent have identified objective indicators of intent. While there is no official list of actions required to objectively indicate your subjective intent to become domiciled in Florida, the following measures have been identified in various court cases as being objective indicators of a person's intent.

We do not suggest that all the steps discussed below are required in order to establish your intent to claim Florida as your legal domicile. However, the more steps you take, the stronger the case that you have established Florida domicile and abandoned your former domicile. Think of it as an apothecary scale and try to tip the scale to one side—Florida Domicile—by taking as many of these following actions as possible:

The Road to Florida Domicile

- File a *declaration of domicile* with the Clerk of Courts in the Florida county where you now reside. (See sample form in Appendix B1.) While a declaration of domicile is not required by Florida, it is a clear indicator of your intent to change your domicile as of the date of the declaration and provides documentary proof of your intent that can be given to others who request such proof.
- Spend as much time in Florida as is practical (preferably more than 180 days per year) and own or lease and occupy a residence in Florida. Most people believe that the Florida test of domicile is spending six months plus one day in Florida. That is not the law in Florida, although the corollary is often true in northern states—if you spend six months plus one day in a northern state—you may be considered domiciled in that state regardless of your intent to be domiciled in Florida. For further information and links to your former state's laws concerning domicile and taxation, see wwmrglaw.com/domicile-information. It is a very strong objective indicator of your intent to be domiciled in Florida if you spend more time in Florida than you spend in any other state.
- Obtain a Florida driver license. For more detailed information about this important step, see Chapter 7.
- Register and license your cars, boats and other vehicles in Florida. See Chapter 7.
- Register to vote in Florida and notify the voting registrar in your former state to remove your name from its voting records. For more information, see Chapter 8.
- If you file your federal income tax returns via mail, do so in the correct location for persons domiciled in Florida. Visit www.irs.gov and search "Where to File" for

correct addresses and situations. If you file your federal income tax return electronically, it will automatically be properly routed provided you use your Florida address on your return.

- File a final income tax return in the state where you were formerly domiciled and mark it as your final return. If you continue to receive income from a source in your former state (e.g., rental income generated by real estate located in your former state), you may be required to file a *nonresident income tax return.*

- Establish relationships with Florida attorneys, doctors, accountants, financial planners, trust officers and insurance agents. In most states, this is a major consideration in domicile disputes. However, to avoid losing business, various professionals have applied pressure to their state legislators to change this. As a result, a few states, the most recent being Minnesota, have enacted legislation to remove from consideration in a domicile dispute—for both income and estate tax purposes—the location of an individual's attorneys, CPAs, financial advisor and bank accounts.

- Transfer financial assets (e.g., securities, bank accounts and brokerage accounts) to institutions in Florida or to financial institutions that maintain offices and do business in Florida.

- Maintain a safe deposit box in Florida rather than in your former state (based on at least one court case, this could be a seemingly insignificant but crucial factor in determining your domicile).

- Transact business from Florida and declare Florida as your state of domicile in all written communications concerning your principal residence. Use your Florida address on all legal documents like deeds, leases, contracts, securities, etc.

- Update your estate-planning documents, such as wills, trusts, living wills, health care designations and powers of attorney, to state that you are domiciled in Florida. Have existing estate-planning documents reviewed by a Florida attorney to be sure that they conform to Florida law.
- Withdraw your membership from non-Florida clubs or institutions where residence in your former state is a prerequisite to membership.
- If you have a professional license issued by your former state (e.g., real estate license, medical license, CPA license, etc.), change your status with the licensing agency to "non-resident," or terminate it, rather than letting it expire.
- If you are a member of a union in your former state, either terminate your membership or transfer your membership to reflect your new Florida domicile.
- Establish affiliations with social and religious organizations in Florida.
- Request a change to nonresident status for organizations (i.e., country clubs, church organizations, etc.) in your former state of domicile—if you plan to maintain those affiliations.
- If you return to your northern state to fish or hunt, purchase a nonresident fishing or hunting license for that purpose.
- Use your Florida address for all correspondence.
- Have all your mail come to Florida, even if you travel back and forth to your former state of residence. Your mail can be forwarded from Florida by the U.S. Postal Service or, for a weekly fee, the Post Office will hold your mail, package it up and ship it to you each week by Priority Mail®. Visit www.usps.com and click forward under the Track & Manage tab. For many, the Priority

Mail service may be a better choice, as the regular U.S.P.S. forwarding service only forwards First Class mail and some important notices, such as notices from the IRS, say "Do Not Forward."

- Change your address on all credit cards, charge accounts, corporations, partnerships and trusts to your Florida address.
- Notify your insurance carriers, including your property and casualty insurer and health insurer, of your change of domicile to Florida.
- Transfer family possessions, paintings, heirlooms and collections to Florida.
- While it is not necessary to own a home, mobile home or condominium in Florida, the commitment to ownership would represent further evidence of your intent. Also, if you change your Florida location frequently (e.g., because you travel around Florida in a motor home), you should establish a place to receive your mail, such as a private mailbox or post office box, in Florida.
- If you own a home in Florida, file for homestead exemption and terminate any homestead exemption on your former home—if you plan to retain that home.
- Change your mobile phone number to a Florida area code. Interestingly, when conducting audits, some states request your mobile phone records in order to determine the number of days spent in their state. Apparently, mobile phones "ping" off of the nearest tower, regardless of whether calls are made or received.
- Celebrate special family occasions in Florida.
- Change your personal online information (e.g., social media profiles) to reflect your new domicile.
- Send out "We Have Moved" cards and keep a list of all the recipients.

- Give up all of the I-Pass or EZ-Pass accounts in your former state.
- If you are paying tuition for one or more members of your family to attend a school in your former state of domicile, that state may take into consideration in a domicile dispute whether you are paying resident or non-resident tuition rates.
- If you are transferred to a nursing home in another state (i.e., after a lengthy illness), be sure to have your family list Florida as your home address.
- If you pass away in another state, the death certificate should reflect Florida as your state of residence.

Important Documents to Have Available in a Domicile Dispute:

- Florida Declaration of Domicile
- Voter registration
- Driver license or alternative Florida ID Card
- Automobile registration
- Proof of Florida Homestead Exemption
- A detailed accounting showing your location during the year(s) in dispute
- Lease agreements, if renting your Florida home
- Mail showing the new Florida address
- Local bank account statements
- Safe deposit box agreement with a local Florida bank
- New estate-planning documents reflecting Florida domicile
- Membership cards/statements from clubs in Florida

- Credit card statements showing significant purchases in Florida
- Medical and veterinary records from Florida health care professionals
- Copies or location of social network profiles citing new Florida residence
- Tax returns, especially the final state tax return of your former state
- Online retail account records (showing items sent to Florida)
- Copy of your "We've Moved" notification with a list of recipients

Important Documents in a Domicile Dispute for Estate Tax Purposes:

- Many of the above listed documents
- Location of death
- Location of burial plot and memorial services
- Domicile/residence listed on the death certificate
- Location of probate (if applicable)
- Trust documents showing Florida as the trust situs

Multiple Domiciles

The loss of tax revenue has prompted many state taxing authorities to assert income and estate tax claims against former residents. As discussed previously, it is constitutionally permissible for more than one state to tax you and your estate on the basis of domicile. Consult an attorney on how to best minimize your exposure to double domicile claims, particularly if you continue to own real estate in another state.

For example, it may be a good idea to form a Family Limited Liability Company or Family Limited Partnership and transfer the real estate located in other states to that entity. It may help avoid unwanted domicile claims and may possibly limit your exposure to state estate or inheritance taxes on those assets (see Chapter 4).

Students

A student seeking Florida residency classification must demonstrate that he or she has established a bona fide domicile in Florida rather than maintaining a temporary residence that is incidental to enrollment in a Florida university. To establish domicile, a student would have to take many of the steps discussed previously, along with some special steps that require establishing and maintaining a legal Florida residence for at least 12 months prior to the first day of classes in the semester for which in-state residency status is sought (see Chapter 12 for more details).

"Split Domicile"

Some prospective Florida residents feel that splitting domicile between themselves and a spouse (commonly known as "split domicile") will allow them to have the best of both worlds. While there are circumstances that could call for splitting domicile, it is generally not advisable. Most people who would like to split domicile are interested in doing so in order to claim a homestead exemption in both states. However, Florida will not allow you to retain your Florida homestead exemption if your spouse is claiming a homestead exemption in another state.

Furthermore, a split domicile raises other important issues. For example, a few states require a married couple to file a joint state income tax return if the couple files a joint federal income tax return. In addition, depending on your timing, a split domicile may limit the amount of your total federal capital gain exclusion (from $500,000 for both spouses to $250,000 for one single spouse) for the sale of a principal residence after one spouse changes his or her domicile and three years have passed before the sale.

If the reason for considering a split domicile is because you and your spouse spend substantial portions of the year apart and obtaining two property tax homestead exemptions is not a motivating factor, be sure to consult with a Florida attorney and carefully consider the potential advantages and disadvantages.

Declaration of Domicile

Assuming you are not going to split your domicile between you and your spouse, both you and your spouse will have to declare Florida domicile on separate declaration of domicile forms. The recommended forms are different from county to county, so be sure to use the one for your new county of domicile. See the sample included in Appendix B1.

Five Essential Actions

When you prepare to establish your domicile in Florida, you will probably wonder which actions to take first. The five actions below are our recommended first steps. They will help save you unnecessary work and make the process easier.

1. **Declare Domicile.** Fill out and file your declaration of domicile form(s) and either mail or deliver the form(s) to the courthouse in the county in which you reside. You can obtain the form from your financial advisor, attorney or the clerk of courts in the county where you reside. Not all counties will accept mailed forms. Also, it may be possible to drop off the declaration at your local Florida Driver License Bureau office. Both you and your spouse should file a declaration. There is a small fee for recording each one-page document. Keep a copy of the filed form and consider stapling a copy to your final state income tax return in your former state of domicile.

2. **Obtain a Driver License.** Obtain your Florida driver license at a Florida Driver License Bureau office in the county in which you declare domicile. For more details on what you will need to bring when you obtain a new license, see Chapter 7.

3. **Register to Vote.** You can register to vote at most Florida Driver License Bureau offices. You may also be able to register at your public library. Learn more about voting in Florida in Chapter 8.

4. **Register Automobile(s).** You should register your automobile(s) and obtain a Florida license plate at the tax collector's office in the county where you reside. For more information, see Chapter 7.

5. **Apply for Homestead Exemption.** If you own rather than rent a home, you can apply for homestead exemption at the property appraiser's office in the county where your home is located. For a list of the items you will need to bring when applying for a Florida homestead exemption, see Chapter 3.

Attention Snowbirds

Many states are becoming aggressive in challenging the domicile status of individuals who claim they are no longer residents of that state but continue to have ties to that state, such as a second home, rental property, a business, etc. Such challenges to your domicile status by your former state of residence can be time consuming, expensive and emotionally draining.

At issue are taxes. With many states suffering from large deficits, it is understandable that they would like to continue to claim you as a resident and tax you on all your income, regardless of where you earn that income. As a nonresident, you are only required to pay income tax to your former state on income sourced in that state.

There is also the question of estate taxes at your death. If your former state has a state estate and/or inheritance tax and you have not properly established your change in domicile to Florida, your heirs may face an unexpected tax from your former state upon your death.

For some taxpayers, the stakes are high. For example, Derek Jeter, the highly paid, retired New York Yankee baseball star, was challenged in 2006 by New York state tax officials who claimed he lived in Florida to avoid paying city and state income taxes for several years, when he was actually living in New York. The claim involved back taxes totaling seven figures. Among the evidence cited by officials were Mr. Jeter's business ties outside Florida, the personal items "near and dear" he kept in his New York apartment, holidays spent in jurisdictions other than Florida and his public statements regarding his desire to be in New York (i.e., "I love New York!"). In attorneys' fees alone, Derek Jeter's failure to pay attention to some of the basic ways to establish his Florida domicile and prove his intent cost him plenty. The total amount Mr. Jeter had to pay is unknown, as the two sides reached an undisclosed settlement in 2007.

A more typical example is Mr. and Mrs. Baker, a couple in their mid-60s who decided to move out of New York and retire in Florida. The Bakers continued to own their New York City home and spent holidays and summers in New York visiting their children and grandchildren who still lived there. The Bakers owned a business for many years and passed most of the responsibilities of the business to their children upon retirement. Their investments provided them with a comfortable retirement in Florida and allowed them to frequently visit New York and travel abroad. Since their retirement, the Bakers had not filed New York tax returns.

Years later, the New York taxing authorities challenged their nonresident status and sought to tax the Bakers as New York State and City residents for income tax purposes. Note: there is no time limit for the State of New York to examine a year for which no return was filed. However, if the Bakers had filed a nonresident return for a year (on income from New York), the State would, generally, only have up to three years from the tax filing due date or when the return was actually filed, whichever is later, to challenge the return. The domicile challenge came as a big surprise to the Bakers and caused them a great deal of time, expense and emotional stress during their fight with the New York state tax officials.

One of the worst parts of fighting a challenge by your former state of residence is that the burden of proof is on you, the taxpayer, to establish your change of domicile. The proof of intent is based on several factors, such as those discussed above, to determine where a taxpayer's true home lies. In this example, the Bakers' family ties weighed against them. Their time spent in New York would also weigh against them if they spent more time in New York than in Florida, as would the extent of any involvement in their family business. New York tax officials may also compare their New York home to their Florida home and consider any valuable or sentimental possessions kept in New York. In a state challenge like this, the analysis is largely subjective and the final judgment of your domicile could rest on how many of the actions on the list of indicators of intent you have completed.

Like many states, New York has specific, objective statutes that would automatically cause them to tax a person as a resident. For example, under New York law, a person is subject to New York taxes for any year in which he or she "maintains a permanent place of abode" (i.e., a second home or rental unit) and spends more than 183 days of the taxable year in New York (typically, any part of a day spent in New York is considered a "New York day"). So, in our example, if the Bakers had access to their New York home and spent more than 183 days in New York, they would likely lose a domicile challenge—regardless of how many other things they had done in an attempt to prove their intent.

With proper planning and attention to details, you can limit your exposure to domicile challenges from your former state. You should prepare in advance for a challenge by keeping records—such as where you spent your time during the year—especially if you frequently visit your previous state of residence. Poor documentation on your part will likely result in ongoing exposure to income taxes and, possibly, state estate taxes at your death, in your former state of residence. Using the apothecary scale analogy, putting more "weight" on the Florida side of the scale, via the action items listed previously, represents the best way to protect yourself from challenges and prove your intent to make Florida your official domicile.

State-Specific Domicile Steps

Unfortunately, there is no official list of specific actions published that, without question, allows you to objectively indicate your subjective intent to become domiciled in Florida. In fact, the measures used to identify a person's intent may vary from state to state.

Fortunately, co-author Brad Galbraith and his law firm, Woods, Weidenmiller, Michetti, Rudnick & Galbraith, PLLC, have built a system on the firm's website that can provide you with information on your former state's specific change-of-domicile requirements.

Visit www.wwmrglaw.com/domicile-information, enter your e-mail address, name and current state of domicile. A member of the WWMR&G estate-planning team will email you links to government website pages that outline any state-specific domicile or change-of-residency requirements.

"I warned him. 'Don't text and drive' ... He wouldn't listen."

Most of American life consists of driving somewhere and then returning home, wondering why the hell you went.
– John Updike

CHAPTER 7

FLORIDA DRIVER LICENSES AND MOTOR VEHICLES

To make your move to Florida complete, you will need to obtain a driver license, register your vehicles and obtain the necessary insurance. There are 129 Tax Collector offices in 46 Florida counties that offer driver license services. By reviewing the steps below, you will find these tasks relatively straightforward to accomplish.

Driver License

If you move to Florida and intend to drive, you must get a Florida driver license within 30 days of becoming a resident. For this purpose, you are considered a resident of Florida if you do any of the following:

- File a Florida declaration of domicile.
- Enroll your children in a Florida public school.
- Register to vote in Florida.
- File for a Florida homestead exemption.

- Accept employment in Florida.
- Reside in Florida for more than six consecutive months.

You do not need a Florida driver license if you have a valid driver license from another state or country and you are:

- A nonresident visitor who is at least sixteen years old.
- A nonresident attending college in Florida.
- Employed by the U.S. government and drive a U.S. government motor vehicle on official business.
- A nonresident working in Florida under a contract for the U.S. government (note: this exemption is valid for 60 days).
- A person who drives only temporarily on the highway (i.e., farm equipment).
- A licensed driver who lives in another state and travels regularly between his or her home and Florida workplace.
- A nonresident migrant farm worker who has a valid license from his or her home state. This is true even if the nonresident migrant farm worker has children in a Florida public school.

If you are a member of the Armed Forces stationed in Florida, you will not need a Florida license except under the following circumstances:

- You or your spouse claim a Florida homestead exemption. In this case, all the drivers in your family must obtain Florida licenses.
- You become employed in Florida. All the drivers in your family must each obtain a Florida driver license.
- Your spouse becomes employed in Florida. Your spouse and children who drive must obtain Florida licenses.

- One or more of your children becomes employed. Only the employed child who drives must obtain a Florida license.

To obtain a Florida driver license or identification (ID) card, you must provide a driver license from another state or country and a second form of identification. Acceptable forms of identification include: social security card, marriage certificate, life insurance policy, a certified copy of your birth certificate or passport. These requirements apply to immigrants as well as nonimmigrants.

Please be aware that Florida does not recognize all out-of-state IDs as a primary form of identification. If you are from one of the 20 states listed below, your identification card will only be acceptable as a second form of identification. In this situation, you will need to present one of the following documents:

- Original or Certified United States birth certificate
- Valid United States passport
- Certificate of Naturalization

These states' driver licenses are not acceptable as a primary form of identification:

- Alaska
- Connecticut
- Hawaii
- Illinois
- Indiana
- Iowa
- Michigan
- Minnesota
- Nebraska
- New Jersey
- North Carolina
- Oregon
- Rhode Island
- Tennessee
- Texas
- Utah
- Vermont
- Virginia
- Washington
- Wisconsin

If you have an out-of-state driver license, you may be able to convert your license without taking a written or road test. You will need to have a vision test—so bring along your glasses or wear your contacts if you need them for driving. Some local driver license offices will allow you to call ahead and schedule an appointment. To locate the nearest driver license office, call the Customer Service Center (statewide) at (850) 617-2000 or find the local phone number online at www.hsmv.state.fl.us/offices.

If you are renewing your license and you are 80 years of age or older, you will be required to complete a vision test. This test must be completed within one year from the date of renewal of a license. You may schedule a free exam at any Florida Driver License Office or with a medical doctor, osteopathic physician or optometrist. If you elect to see a doctor outside the Florida Driver License Office, that doctor must complete the Mature Driver Vision Test Form (HSMV72119).

On January 1, 2010, Florida enacted new documentation requirements for residents renewing or obtaining a new driver license or identification card. Called "Gather, Go, Get," you must bring original documents that prove your identity, social security number and residential address. The best way to determine which documents you will need to bring is to go to the website www.gathergoget.com and follow their checklist instructions. Alternately, if you fail to bring the correct documentation when you arrive at a Florida driver license office, an agent will explain which documents they will require for when you return.

Florida Identification (ID) Card

If you do not drive, you can obtain a Florida identification card at any Florida driver license office. If you are 60 years of age or older, the card is good for life; otherwise, it is valid for four years. Similar to a Florida driver license, the ID card will contain such things as your name, address, date of birth and color photograph. To obtain the ID card, you must meet the following criteria:

- Be five years of age or older and have a Social Security number. (Note: certain counties have no minimum age requirement and any person can be issued an identification card if applying for a disabled parking permit.)
- Present your official Social Security card (issued by the Social Security Administration).
- Present one other form of identification (e.g., either an original or a certified copy of your birth certificate or your passport).

Canadian Citizens

Under federal law, Canadian citizens are nonimmigrants and are allowed to stay in the United States without obtaining U.S. Citizenship and Immigration Services (CIS) documentation. Canadians without such documentation must provide proof of Canadian citizenship to be issued a Florida driver license or identification card by presenting any two of the following:

- A Canadian driver license,
- An original or certified copy of the Canadian birth certificate,
- A Canadian passport and/or
- A Canadian naturalization certificate.

If you are not a Canadian citizen but have a Canadian driver license, you are required to provide the same proof of legal presence as any other non-U.S. citizen.

First Time Drivers

If you are seeking a Florida driver license and have never been issued a license in any state or country, you will be required to complete a traffic law and substance abuse education course as a prerequisite for obtaining a Florida driver license.

There are various course options available to satisfy the substance abuse education requirement, including an online course offered in association with the American Safety Council at www.firsttimedriver.com.

Changes to Your Driver License

If your address or name changes, you are required to obtain a new license showing your new address or name change within 10 days of that change. Be sure to bring a court order or marriage license to the Florida driver license office for proof of any name change.

If you are an immigrant and have legally changed your name by marriage or court order, you must have your name changed on your U.S. Citizenship and Immigration Services (CIS) documents. A receipt from CIS indicating Form I-90 (Green Card) has been filed for a name change is acceptable for a name change on your driver license or identification card.

If you are Canadian and have legally changed your name by marriage or court order, you must have your name changed on your Canadian license and/or passport before applying for a name change on your Florida driver license or identification card.

Renewals, Duplicates or Replacements

Any immigrant or nonimmigrant holding a Florida driver license or identification card who needs a renewal, duplicate or replacement driver license or identification card must apply in person at a driver license office and present his or her identification documents as described above.

Motor Vehicle Insurance Laws

Florida law requires you to have motor vehicle insurance that meets the following criteria:

- Your insurance must be written as Florida coverage.
- Whichever company issues your Florida policy must be an insurance company licensed by the Florida Office of Insurance Regulation.
- Any person who has a motor vehicle in Florida for more than 90 days (consecutive or not) during a 365-day period must be covered under a personal injury protection and property damage liability insurance policy.

You must maintain the required minimum coverage (see the sections on Financial Responsibility Law and No-Fault Law, below) at all times for the vehicles you register.

To protect its citizens, Florida has two important insurance laws: the Financial Responsibility Law and the No-Fault Law. You should understand these laws because, unless you have the proper insurance, you could lose your driver license and vehicle registration tag and may have to pay substantial fees to have them reinstated.

The Financial Responsibility Law (FRL) requires owners and operators of motor vehicles to be financially responsible for damages and/or injuries they may cause to others when a motor vehicle accident happens in Florida. The FRL requires any licensed person to have either the following minimum liability insurance or to post a bond or cash that guarantees responsibility for the following minimum limits:

- $10,000 bodily injury liability (BIL),
- $20,000 bodily injury liability to two or more persons,
- $10,000 property damage liability (PDL) or
- $30,000 combined single limits.

The above is often referred to as the 10/20/10 requirements and there are penalties if there is an accident and the vehicle operator does not meet these minimums. The penalties include the suspension of the driver license of the operator and the registrations of all vehicles of the owner.

If you are involved in any of the following violations and you do not have insurance that complies with the FRL, your driver license and/or vehicle registration tag can be suspended for up to three years:

- A crash where you were at fault;
- A suspension for too many points against your driver license;
- A citation for driving under the influence (DUI) of alcohol or controlled/chemical substances which results in a revocation;
- A revocation for being a "habitual traffic offender;" or
- A revocation for any serious offense where the Florida Department of Highway Safety and Motor Vehicles is required to revoke your license.

In addition, if you are the driver or the owner of a vehicle which is in a crash that is your fault, the Florida Department of Highway Safety and Motor Vehicles may require you to pay for some or all of the damages before your driving privileges are reinstated.

The No-Fault Law requires anyone who owns or has registered a motor vehicle with four or more wheels (excluding limousines and taxis) that has been in the state for 90 days or more (consecutive or not) during the past 365 days to have a Florida insurance policy with the following minimum coverages:

- $10,000 of personal injury protection (PIP) and
- $10,000 of property damage liability (PDL).

Proper Florida insurance coverage, based on the above laws, is necessary before you can register your car or other four-wheel vehicle. In addition, your insurance company must notify the Department of Highway Safety and Motor Vehicles if you renew, fail to renew or cancel your Florida policy.

In other words, you must maintain Florida insurance coverage the entire time your vehicle is registered in your name. You must turn in the registration and license tag at any Florida Driver License Office or the Department of Highway Safety and Motor Vehicles (via mail) if you cancel the insurance, place the vehicle in storage or if the vehicle is not in working order.

The Florida Department of Highway Safety and Motor Vehicle Bureau of Motorist Compliance, 2900 Apalachee Parkway, Room B260F, MS-87, Tallahassee, Florida 32399-0585 (www.hsmv.state.fl.us/ddl/frfaqcrash.html), was created to ensure that everyone is accountable for their actions involving motor vehicles. In the unfortunate event that you are involved in an accident, you will be either directly or indirectly dealing with this organization as it will eventually be reviewing the accident. The Bureau of Motorist Compliance has considerable power and authority and could suspend an at-fault party's license for up to 20 years.

Proof of Insurance

Insurance companies licensed to do business in Florida will issue you an insurance certificate or ID card. You must have this certificate or ID card ready to show to any police officer to prove that you have the required insurance. If not, you may be ticketed for not having proof of insurance.

Alternatively, you may obtain a self-insurance certificate from

Tickets, Tickets, Tickets

In 2016 alone, uniformed police officers wrote more than $1.3 million in traffic violations, creating massive earnings for the state. In fact, the Florida Department of Highway Safety and Motor Vehicles collected nearly $2.3 billion in fiscal year 2015/2016 from fees, fines and titles.

Source: *flhsmv.gov.*

Florida's Top 9 Saltwater Game Fish

Saltwater fishing is an all-time favorite for both residents and visitors. The miles of coastline make saltwater fishing a family sport or an individual leisure activity. Florida's top nine saltwater game fish, their size and seasons are:

Cobia:	33-inch min. size; no closed season, 1 per day
Dolphinfish:	No min. size limit; no closed season, 10 per person
Grouper:	Gag and Black: 22-inch minimum size; Red and Scamp: 20-inch minimum size. Seasons change frequently, consult FWC
King Mackerel:	24-inch min. size; no closed season, 2 per person
Redfish:	18 to 27 inches; no closed season
Sea Trout:	15 to 20 inches; no closed season
Snapper:	Size depends on species; Seasons change frequently, consult FWC.
Snook:	Atlantic: 28 to 32 inches; Open Feb-May and Sept-Dec 15th. Gulf: 28 to 33 inches; Open March, April, Sept-Nov.
Tarpon:	No min. size limit; catch and release, 1 per person

According to the Florida Fish and Wildlife Conservation Commission, children under the age of 16 and Florida resident seniors who are 65 or older are not required to purchase a fishing license. However, be aware that officers may ask children and seniors for proof of age. Seniors should also be prepared to show proof of residency, such as a driver license.

Nonresidents—including visitors over 65—need to have a Florida hunting license and permits and/or a recreational fishing license and permits, unless fishing with a charter captain or from a licensed pier.

the Bureau of Financial Responsibility by either depositing cash or securities with the department or by providing satisfactory proof of financial responsibility.

Insurance Types

The typical motor vehicle insurance policy has several separate components.

Personal injury protection (PIP) compensates for a loss regardless of who is charged with causing the automobile accident. PIP applies to bodily injury to you, relatives who live in your home, other passengers of your vehicle and licensed drivers who drive your vehicle with your permission. PIP insurance also protects you if you are injured as a pedestrian or bicyclist as long as the injury is caused by a motor vehicle.

Bodily injury liability (BIL) pays for serious injury or death to others when you or a member of your family who lives with you causes an accident involving your or someone else's automobile. Your insurance company will pay for injuries up to the limits of your policy and provide legal representation for you if you get sued. It may also cover others who drive your automobile with your permission.

The purchase of BIL is optional if you post a bond or cash that guarantees responsibility for the 10/20/10 limits. However, if you have been convicted of certain driving offenses and/or have been in an accident, you may be required to purchase BIL coverage.

Property damage liability (PDL) pays for damages to other people's property for which you or members of your family are liable in a crash involving a motor vehicle.

Factors Affecting Personal Insurance Rates

Motor vehicle insurance rates in Florida can be affected by a number of factors:

- Your age and gender
- Your driving history
- The type and age of automobile you drive
- The value of the automobile you drive
- The existence of antitheft devices on your vehicle
- The distance you drive to work
- The number of years you have had your driver license
- The existence of safety devices on your vehicle
- The geographic area in which the automobile will be used

Information Sources

For additional insurance information, such as a list of insurance companies licensed to do business in Florida and motor vehicle requirements, contact the Office of Insurance Regulation at (850) 413-3140 or the Florida Department of Highway Safety and Motor Vehicles online at www.flhsmv.gov.

VEHICLES

Titling a Motor Vehicle in Florida

To title your motor vehicle in Florida, you must complete an application for certificate of title that is available at any office of the Department of Highway Safety and Motor Vehicles. Alternatively, you may obtain the application online at www.flhsmv.gov. After obtaining and completing the form, mail it and your proof of insurance to your local county tax collector office.

If a vehicle is in joint ownership with "and" or "or" between the two names, both signatures are required on the application for Florida title.

When the title is held by a lien holder in a different state, the local tax collector's office will assist you in getting the original sent to Florida. After the Florida title is issued with the recorded lien, it will be returned to the lien holder. A list of Florida tax collectors is available by visiting floridarevenue.com and searching "tax collectors."

Before a Florida title can be issued, the vehicle identification number (VIN) of the vehicle must be verified. The VIN can be verified by one of the following people on Form HSMV 82042:

- A county tax collector employee or Division of Motor Vehicle compliance examiner;
- A law enforcement officer from any state;
- A licensed dealer from Florida;
- A provost marshal or commissioned officer in active military service, with a rank of second lieutenant or higher; or
- A Florida Notary.

Home of the Smallest

Florida is home to both the smallest police station and the smallest post office in the United States.

The smallest post office is located in Ochopee and is a popular attraction. After a fire in 1953 destroyed the existing post office, postal workers moved into the tool shed behind the office as a temporary spot. Not even Hurricane Irma could bring it down in 2017. The tiny building serves 1,500 local residents of which about 900 are Native Americans.

The smallest police station is in a phone booth in Carrabelle. Because the town was small, the station was just a phone booth near a building. Since 1963, it keeps officers out of the rain.

Form HSMV 82042 must be completed and signed by the vehicle owner and the person performing the VIN verification. The form is available from your local tax collector's office or the website of the Florida Department of Highway Safety and Motor Vehicles.

To expedite the process of re-titling and registering your out-of-state vehicle in Florida, drive your vehicle and bring your proof of insurance to any office of the Department of Highway Safety and Motor Vehicles. As part of the process, a department employee will accompany you to your vehicle to verify the VIN.

Following is a list of vehicles exempt from VIN verification:

- New vehicles when a manufacturer's certificate of origin is submitted (regardless of location purchase)
- Mobile homes
- Trailers or semitrailers with a net weight of less than 2,000 pounds
- Travel trailers
- Camp trailers
- Truck campers
- Fifth-wheel recreation trailers

Registering Motor Vehicles

In Florida, a motor vehicle is required by law to be registered within 10 days of the owner either becoming employed, placing children in public school or establishing residency.

Unless a motor vehicle is exempt from titling (such as mopeds, motorized bicycles and trailers weighing less than 2,000 pounds), it must be titled in Florida at the same time it is registered. You can accomplish both actions by completing an application for certificate of title and registration, as noted above, and submitting the documents by mail or in person at the local county tax collector's

Festival Florida

Whatever your interest, Florida has a popular event to match it. Here are some of the standouts:

Bike Week: Every spring and fall, motorcycle enthusiasts congregate in Daytona Beach to celebrate the biking culture.

Florida Folk Festival: Over almost a 60-year history, the Florida Folk Festival has celebrated the best folk music with some big names. The festival is held in the Stephen Foster Folk Culture Center State Park in White Springs, FL.

Pirate Festivals: Several cities, including Tampa's famous Gasparilla Pirate Invasion in January, Clearwater and Key West, host swashbuckling weekends complete with tall ships, parades, marathons, costumes and piratical reenactments.

Film Festivals: Becoming increasingly popular are boutique film festivals around Florida. Most feature up-and-coming filmmakers and typically include several dinner or special screening events. Attend one in Sarasota, Naples, Orlando or Fort Lauderdale.

Florida Renaissance Festival: Browse through enchanted craft villages, applaud hundreds of period performers, cheer valiant knights, enjoy entertainment and food fit for a king. Five weekends every spring in Deerfield Beach.

Florida Seafood Festival: Enjoy delectable seafood and local crafts at this Apalachicola tradition. A parade, oyster eating and shucking contests and the blessing of the fishing fleet highlight the weekend.

Florida Strawberry Festival: Since 1930, this famous Plant City festival has hosted parades, home cooking, marching bands and crafts, every February – all in celebration of the strawberry.

The Florida Sea Cow

Manatees are a well-known Florida animal. These slow-moving mammals live in both fresh- and saltwater, eating aquatic vegetation. The biggest cause of manatee mortality is motorboat propellers. Too slow to move away, they can be maimed or killed. The well-known manatee-theme Florida license plate helped to raise awareness and protect manatees. On average, revenue from the license plate and a special decorative sticker provides over $1.3 million annually for the Save the Manatee Trust Fund.

Florida manatees like shallow, slow-moving rivers, bays, estuaries and coastal water ecosystems. They prefer waters that are about three to seven feet deep. Their habitat provides natural shelter where they enjoy a steady, easily obtainable food supply.

In the winter, manatees seek warmer waters, like springs and warm-water discharges at power plants. That is the best time to see a manatee. Favorite manatee-watching spots include Blue Springs State Park, the Tampa Electric Company (TECO), Lee County Manatee Park and Merritt Island National Wildlife Refuge. Many Florida aquariums also display rehabbing manatees.

Source: *myfwc.com, savethemanatee.org.*

Reprinted with permission of www.Bigstock.com

office or license plate agency. When you do, you must submit the original title and proof of Florida insurance. If not taken care of previously, a county tax collector employee must verify the VIN at this time.

Registration is for a 12-month period which begins the first day of the owner's birth month. Company-owned vehicles use the month of June. The full amount of the registration fee is charged for the registration period regardless of when, during the registration period, the vehicle is registered. When your vehicle is registered, Florida law requires the registration certificate or an official copy to be in the possession of the operator of the motor vehicle or carried in the vehicle at all times. You must produce this for law enforcement personnel upon demand. If you fail to have this certificate or if your certificate is out of date, the officer may give you a ticket.

Vehicle Transfer Tax

Florida's six percent use tax is due on any vehicle owned less than six months with an out-of-state title that is then brought into Florida. If you purchased a vehicle outside Florida and bring it into Florida within six months, a credit is permitted against your Florida tax obligation for any tax paid on the purchase in another state. However, Florida does not credit any tax paid to another country. Thus, if the vehicle is purchased in another country, the full amount

Government at a Glance

Number of counties in Florida: 67
Form of government: Governor and independent cabinet consisting of three elected state executives: the attorney general, chief financial officer and commissioner of agriculture
Legislature: 120 House districts, 40 Senate districts, 27 Congressional districts

of use tax (6 percent) applies and is due. It does not matter if the motor vehicle was used in that country for a period of six months or more prior to the time it is brought into Florida.

About Cell Phone Use

It is not illegal in Florida to talk on your cell phone while driving but that does not make it safe. Distracted driving is one of the leading causes of accidents in Florida. Although this action cannot cause you to lose your license or receive a ticket, it may lead to actions that can.

Research cited by the Florida Department of Highway Safety and Motor Vehicles states that drivers who talk on the phone while driving are four times more likely to be involved in an accident and those who text message while driving are 23 times more likely. Interestingly, the research showed no improvement in the driving of those using hands-free devices to make calls or texts. The Florida Department of Highway Safety and Motor Vehicles recommends that you always make sure that driving is your first and main priority, keep your eyes on the road and use common sense.

Florida, as well as a large majority of states, prohibits texting while driving. As a secondary offense, however, drivers must be stopped for a separate alleged traffic violation before being ticketed for texting while driving.

Miscellaneous Information

Other Services: The office of Florida Motor Vehicle Services/ County Tax Collector can help you with registration, tag and title for trailers, watercraft and mobile homes. Also, the county tax collector can issue specialty tags and disability parking permits. Currently, Florida offers more than 120 specialty tags, benefitting a variety of causes and charitable organizations.

SunPass: SunPass is Florida's statewide prepaid toll program for use on most Florida toll roads. SunPass can save you time and money and eliminate your wait at Florida toll plazas. Find registration information online at www.sunpass.com.

Driver Records and Privacy Issues: Most Florida motor vehicle and driver license records are subject to public disclosure. The Driver Privacy Protection Act allows you to keep your personal information private by limiting access to this information.

Find additional information about this online at www.flhsmv.gov and search "Driver Privacy Protection Act." Topics include driver licenses, vehicle tags, registration, insurance issues and traffic school.

BOATS

Registration and Title

If you own and operate a motorboat (or any non-motor-powered vessel longer than sixteen feet) on Florida's public waterways, you must register it at the local county tax collector's office.

So Close to Cuba

Key West is home of the southernmost point of the continental United States. Here you will find mile marker 0 which is in the shape of a buoy. From that point, Cuba is only 90 miles away.

Reprinted with permission of www.Bigstock.com

When you purchase a boat, either new or used, you have 30 days to apply for registration and title through the county tax collector's office. During this grace period, you must keep a bill of sale with proof of the date of purchase aboard the watercraft. Operation of an unregistered vessel after 30 days is a second-degree misdemeanor.

As the vessel owner, you must file applications for watercraft registration and title certificates with the county tax collector's office, either in the county where the watercraft is located or in the county where you (the vessel owner) reside.

Unless a vessel is exempt from titling, it must be titled at the same time it is registered. You can accomplish both actions by completing Form HSMV 82040 (available from your local tax collector's office). Along with the completed form, a manufacturer's statement of origin, or its equivalent, must be submitted with the applicable registration fees.

In addition, if the sales tax on the total purchase price of the vessel has not already been paid, the owner must pay the tax in Florida. If the sales tax has been paid, then the vessel owner must provide the county tax collector with a valid receipt indicating where the sales tax was paid and that it was paid in an amount equal to or greater than the applicable Florida sales tax.

SUGARCANE

Sugarcane is a tropical grass that is grown throughout Florida. In many areas of the state, sugarcane is grown only as a hobby crop for syrup production or as a source of "chewing cane." Sugarcane is also grown commercially for the production of crystal or "white" sugar primarily along the shores of Lake Okeechobee. Palm Beach County accounts for approximately 70 percent of the commercial sugarcane acreage. Most of the remainder is grown in Hendry, Glades and Martin Counties.

Source: *Institute of Food and Agriculture, University of Florida.*

Visitors

It is not necessary to register a watercraft in Florida if it is in Florida for 90 days or less and has a current out-of-state registration.

Vessels Exempt from Registration

- Non-motor-powered vessels
- Vessels used exclusively on private lakes and ponds
- Vessels owned by the U.S. government
- Vessels used exclusively as a ship's lifeboat

Vessels Exempt from Titling

- Non-motor-powered vessels less than 16 feet in length
- Federally documented vessels
- Vessels used exclusively on private lakes and ponds
- Amphibious vessels for which a vehicle title is issued by the Department of Highway Safety and Motor Vehicles
- Vessels used solely for demonstration, testing or sales promotional purposes by a dealer or manufacturer
- Vessels owned and operated by the state or its political subdivisions
- Vessels from a country, other than the U.S., temporarily using the waters of Florida for not more than 90 days
- Vessels already covered by registration numbers awarded according to a federally approved numbering system of another state or by the U.S. Coast Guard in a state without a federally approved numbering system, provided that the vessels are not operated in Florida waters more than 90 consecutive days

Transfer of Title to a Vessel

Under Florida law, you may not sell, assign or transfer a vessel titled in Florida without delivering to the purchaser/transferee a valid certificate of title, verifying transfer to the new owner.

You may not purchase or otherwise acquire a vessel that requires titling by the state without obtaining a certificate of title for it in your name. Florida law requires you to file, as the purchaser or transferee, an application for a title transfer within 30 days with the county tax collector of the county where the vessel is located or where you, the new owner, reside and pay the required service fees.

When an application for transfer of ownership is filed with the county tax collector, the purchaser or transferee must surrender the last title document issued for the vessel, after it has been properly executed, to the county tax collector. In addition, the new owner must pay the applicable sales tax on the total purchase price or provide proof of sales tax payment. For answers to other questions or for specific instructions regarding the transfer of ownership based on other factors, such as prior federal documentation, probate or contractual default, contact your local Florida county tax collector's office.

Registration Numbers

The Florida registration number issued to a vessel is permanent and remains with the vessel as long as it is operated or stored in Florida. This is true even if the vessel is sold or transferred.

The registration number issued to an undocumented vessel must be painted or permanently attached to both sides of the bow (front half) of the vessel and must be in block letters and numerals at least 3 inches high. The registration number must read from left to right, contrast in color with the hull and be maintained in legible condition.

The prefix and suffix must be separated from the numerals by a space equal to the width of the digits (e.g., "FL 0017 MK").

Decals

A decal signifying the year during which the registration certificate is valid is issued with each registration certificate. The decal must be displayed on the port (left) side of the vessel immediately before or after the registration number. If issued to a federally documented vessel, the decal may be affixed to a window or windshield on the port side. Remove the decal for a previous year's registration before affixing and displaying the new one.

Out-of-State Registration

Florida recognizes valid registration certificates and numbers issued to visiting vessel owners by other states for 90 days. If you plan to use your vessel in Florida longer than 90 days, you must register it with a county tax collector. However, you may retain the out-of-state registration number if you intend to return to your home state within a reasonable period of time. If you have any questions, check with your county tax collector's office.

Out-of-state vessel owners who plan to remain permanently in Florida must notify the county tax collector. You will then receive a Florida registration certificate number to replace those issued by your former state. You must surrender the out-of-state registration and certificate of title, if issued, to the tax collector.

Out-of-state registration certificates and numbers for vessels owned by military personnel on active duty in Florida are valid in Florida until the expiration date, after which the vessels must be registered by Florida.

AIRCRAFT

If you own or plan to purchase an airplane or helicopter, there are a few things you should know if you intend to operate and/or store your aircraft in Florida.

Registration

Aircraft operated in Florida must be registered in accordance with the regulations of the Federal Aviation Administration. Florida does not require a separate state registration of aircraft.

Tax Issues

In Florida, tax compliance is an important aspect of aircraft ownership. Tax dollars are used toward airport construction,

GEOGRAPHY: NORTHEAST FLORIDA

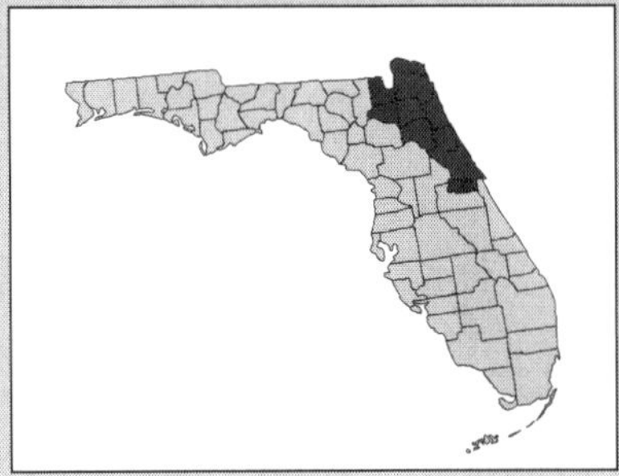

Florida's northeast boundaries stretch from Jacksonville south to Cape Canaveral. The major cities in northeast Florida are Jacksonville, Daytona Beach and St. Augustine. Surfers and sunbathers alike are drawn to this region's famous beaches. It's even possible to drive on the beach in Daytona Beach. St. Augustine offers historic tours and shopping and is also home to the St. Augustine Alligator Farm where you can see all 23 species of crocodilians on display. The Ron Jon Surf Shop in Cocoa Beach is billed as the largest surf shop in the world. Space enthusiasts might catch a launch at the Kennedy Space Center or experience simulated astronaut training at Cape Canaveral.

Facts About Northeast Florida

St. Augustine (founded in 1565) is the oldest European settlement in North America.

Nearly 80 percent of the U.S. intake of sweet Atlantic white shrimp is harvested in Amelia Island waters. Two million pounds of shrimp are delivered to Fernandina docks annually.

The first graded road built in Florida was Old Kings Road in 1763. It was named for King George of England.

During the 1991 Gulf War, the busiest military port in the country was Jacksonville. From this location, the military moved more supplies and people than from any other port in the country.

When completed in 1989, the Dames Point Bridge became the longest cable-stayed span in the United States, the longest concrete span of its type in the Western Hemisphere and the third longest cable-stayed bridge in the world.

The longest river sailboat race in the world is the Annual Mug Race. The event runs 42 miles from Palatka to Jacksonville along the St. Johns River.

Don't miss the Annual Azalea Festival in Palatka and see the town's signature shrubs in many shades of pink and white.

Titusville, known as Space City, USA, is located on the west shore of the Indian River directly across from the John F. Kennedy Space Center.

Source: *www.50states.com/facts/florida.htm.*

improvements to runways and various other necessary services to benefit aircraft owners.

Sales Tax

All aircraft sold and/or delivered in Florida are subject to Florida's 6 percent sales tax, unless the transaction is specifically exempt by law, as discussed below. Florida aircraft dealers and brokers are required to collect sales tax from the purchaser at the time of sale or delivery.

If the aircraft is delivered into a county that imposes a discretionary sales surtax, then the dealer or broker must collect this tax. Discretionary sales surtax applies only to the first $5,000 of the aircraft purchase price. All sales of aircraft between individuals are fully taxable if the sale and/or delivery occurs in Florida.

Trade-Ins

If a sale and trade-in are included in a single transaction, the trade-in allowance may be deducted from the selling price. Thus, only the net sales price is subject to Florida sales tax and applicable discretionary surtax.

Use Tax

Use tax is a component of Florida's sales and use tax law which provides uniform taxation of items, such as airplanes, which may be purchased outside Florida but used, hangared or stored in Florida. Use tax is due on purchases made out of the state and brought into Florida within six months of the purchase date.

Aircraft purchased and used outside Florida for more than six months are generally exempt when brought into Florida if the two following conditions are met:

- The owner has owned the aircraft for more than six months and
- The owner has used the aircraft in another state or states, U.S. territory or District of Columbia for six months or longer prior to bringing the aircraft to Florida.

To report use tax due to Florida on the purchase of an aircraft, the purchaser should complete an ownership declaration and sales and use tax report on aircraft (Form DR-42A). See below for information on obtaining this and other forms.

Tax Credits for Purchases Outside Florida

Florida allows credit for sales or use taxes lawfully imposed and paid to another state, U.S. territory or the District of Columbia if the aircraft later becomes subject to Florida tax.

Florida does not allow credit for taxes paid to a foreign country and will not recognize use in a foreign country for any length of time. Any aircraft imported from a foreign country to Florida for use, distribution or storage (with the intent to be used in Florida) is subject to Florida's use tax.

Ramp Checks (Visual Inspections)

To ensure that the appropriate tax has been paid on aircraft operated or stored in Florida, the Florida Department of Revenue periodically conducts ramp checks, which are visual inspections at Florida airports and fixed-base operation facilities.

Information and Forms

For detailed responses to your additional concerns and questions, contact:

Aircraft Enforcement Unit
Florida Department of Revenue
PO Box 6417
Tallahassee, FL 32314-6417
Telephone: (850) 487-3273
Fax: (850) 487-0969
www.myflorida.com/dor

To speak with a Department of Revenue representative, call Taxpayer Services, Monday through Friday, 8 a.m. to 7 p.m. ET, at (800) 352-3671.

Persons with hearing or speech impairments may call the TDD line at (800) 367-8331 or (850) 922-1115.

Any of the following methods will allow you to receive forms by mail:

- Order multiple copies of forms from www.myflorida.com/dor/forms.
- Fax form requests to the DOR Distribution Center at (850) 922-2208.
- Mail form requests to:

  Distribution Center
  Florida Department of Revenue
  168A Blountstown Highway
  Tallahassee, FL 32304-2702

QUESTIONS AND ANSWERS

Vehicle Registration

Q: What is a registration?

A: A registration is evidence of having paid the registration tax and fees on a motor vehicle. It consists of a metal license plate, a validation decal and a registration certificate.

Q: How do I register a vehicle if I am out of state?

A: If registering a vehicle from out of state, complete the application for Certificate of Title found at flhsmv.gov/dmv/forms/BTR/82040.pdf. Mail the completed form and fee ($100) to your local Florida county tax collector or license plate agency.

Q: How do I register a vehicle if I am in Florida?

A: If registering a vehicle in person, submit the original title and proof of Florida insurance to the local county tax collector or license plate agency.

Bump into Vanity

Florida helped start the specialty license plate craze in 1986 when it issued a commemorative plate of the space shuttle Challenger. Since then, Florida has developed over 120 themed plates, many of which support various causes from universities and conservation to sports teams and charities.

One of the most popular Florida specialty plates is the "Protect the Panther" plate. A portion of funds from the sale of these plates helps panther research and conservation.

Q: If I don't register my vehicle on time, is there a delinquent fee?

A: Section 320.07(4)(a), Florida Statutes, specifically requires the delinquent fee to be imposed on any applicant who fails to renew a registration before the end of the month in which renewal registration is due.

The delinquent fee is applied beginning on the eleventh calendar day of the month succeeding the renewal period. The exact expiration date is shown on the current registration certificate. Therefore, the registered owner should be well aware of when his or her registration expires.

Q: Why must out-of-state residents have Florida proof of insurance before obtaining a license plate or registration renewal?

A: Florida insurance is necessary to meet the requirements of Florida statutes. Only insurance issued or countersigned by a Florida agent is electronically reported to the Department of Highway Safety and Motor Vehicles for verification purposes.

Q: Do I carry the registration with me or in the car?

A: Section 320.0605, Florida Statutes, requires the registration certificate or an official copy to be in the possession of the operator of the motor vehicle or carried in the vehicle at all times. Therefore, either way is permissible as long as you can produce a copy for law enforcement upon demand.

Q: What are the basic registration fees?

A: Registration rates, subject to statutory change, are shown in the table on page 159.

Q: How do I register my motorcycle, scooter or moped?

A: Information for registering motorcycles, scooters and mopeds is contained in the DMV Procedures Manual, procedure number RS-61. For registration fees for motorcycles and mopeds, it is best to contact your local driver license office.

Classification	Weight	Annual Tax & Other Fees
Automobiles (private use)	up to 2499 lbs.	$19.50
	2500 - 3499 lbs.	$30.50
	3500 lbs. or greater	$44.00
Trucks (private & commercial)	up to 1999 lbs.	$19.50
	2000 - 3000 lbs.	$30.50
	3001 - 5000 lbs.	$44.00

For registration fees for motorcycles, mopeds, mobile homes, trailers and others, call your local tax collector's office or visit your local tax collector's website.

Pioneers in Transportation

Railroad barons helped make Florida what it is today. One of the best known tycoons was Henry Flagler. A prototypical businessman, real estate investor and partner in Standard Oil, Flagler developed the East Coast Railway after visiting and falling in love with St. Augustine. Like other railroad men, he also built a lavish hotel, the Ponce de León Hotel, to attract tourists.

One of the major Southwest Florida roads is the Tamiami Trail, running from Tampa to Miami. When tourism and industry started to boom in the 1920s, Barron G. Collier helped fund the building and paving of the trail. In return, the State Legislature created Collier County. Tamiami Trail officially opened in 1928. When Collier died in 1939, he was the largest landowner in Florida.

Title

Q: What is a title?

A: A certificate of title is the proof of ownership of a motor vehicle in the state of Florida. Most vehicles are required to be titled. The exceptions are mopeds, motorized bicycles and trailers weighing less than 2,000 pounds.

Q: When must I apply for title?

A: When, as a Florida resident, you purchase a new motor vehicle or bring one into the state or change the ownership, you must apply for a title in your name.

Q: What do I need as proper proof of insurance?

A: Proof of personal injury protection (PIP) and property damage liability (PDL) insurance may be shown using the original or a photocopy of one of the following:

- Florida automobile insurance identification card,
- Florida insurance policy,
- Certificate of insurance or
- An original affidavit signed by the insured, giving the name of the insurance company, policy number, type of insurance coverage and the description of the vehicle.

Q: What must I have to apply for registration and title?

A: You must have proof of ownership and proof of required insurance coverage written or countersigned by a Florida agent. Next, you must purchase or transfer your license plate. Be sure to record a lien if the vehicle is financed. Then you have to complete and sign the appropriate title application form and pay sales tax, title and registration fees.

Q: Where can I apply for registration and title?

A: Application for registration and title to a motor vehicle can be made at any of the tax collector or license plate agencies located in each of the counties throughout Florida.

Q: If the vehicle is purchased by joint ownership, why do both parties have to be present?

A: If a vehicle is purchased by joint ownership with "and" or "or" between the two names, both signatures are required on the application for Florida title, per Section 319.22, Florida Statutes.

Q: Why is sales tax collected if the vehicle has been owned less than six months on an out-of-state title?

A: Florida state law requires that sales tax be collected in Florida for a vehicle owned less than six months on an out-of-state title. The money is actually collected as use tax instead of sales tax.

Miscellaneous

Q: Is it legal to talk on my cell phone while driving?

A: Yes. It is perfectly legal to talk on a cell phone while driving in Florida but that doesn't mean you should. One of the biggest causes of accidents in Florida is distracted drivers.

Q: Is it legal to text on my cell phone or other personal device while driving?

A: Florida, as well as a large majority of states, prohibits texting while driving. It is a secondary offense, however, as drivers must be stopped for a separate alleged traffic violation before being ticketed for texting while driving.

Q: Are points given for a texting offense?

A: There are no points for the first offense. Two points are added to the primary offense (e.g., speeding) if texting occurred in a school zone. Six points are added if the texting offense resulted in a crash.

"Oh yeah? Well, I'm offering a 700 billion dollar tax cut AND a free tote bag!"

A man without a vote is a man without protection.
– Lyndon B. Johnson

CHAPTER 8

REGISTERING TO VOTE IN FLORIDA

You may vote in any Florida election that applies to your Florida city or county if you are registered to vote. To register, you must:

- Be a citizen of the United States of America,
- Be a Florida citizen/resident,
- Be eighteen years old (you may preregister if you are seventeen),
- Not have been adjudicated mentally incapacitated with respect to voting in Florida or any other state,
- Not have been convicted of a felony unless your civil rights have been restored,
- Have a current, valid Florida driver license number or Florida identification card number; if you don't have either, you must provide the last four digits of your Social Security Number and
- Not claim the right to vote in another state.

How to Register

You can register to vote at your local county Supervisor of Elections office. Alternatively, you can register at any Florida driver license office. A driver license examiner will ask you if you would like to apply for voter registration or change your address or party affiliation and provide you with an application of registration at the time you receive your license. Your voter registration application is then forwarded to your local county Supervisor of Elections office. Your official registration card will be mailed to you by your local county Supervisor of Elections office.

You may apply for voter registration online by downloading the form at dos.myflorida.com/elections and clicking "Register to Vote or Update your Info" under the resources tab. Simply fill out, print and sign the online Florida voter registration application form. Using the address provided, mail the application to your county Supervisor of Elections or hand-deliver the signed form to a Florida driver license office, a voter registration agency, an armed forces recruitment office, the Florida Division of Elections or to any Florida office of the Supervisor of Elections.

The date your completed application is postmarked or hand-delivered to a voter registration agency will be your registration date. You must be registered at least 29 days before you can vote in an election.

If your application is complete and you qualify as a voter, the Supervisor of Elections will mail you a voter information card. You may call your county Supervisor of Elections if you have not received your card within eight weeks or if you have any questions.

Florida is a closed primary state. If you wish to register to vote in a partisan primary election, you must be a registered voter in the party for which the primary is being held. Your Florida application form has a place to make your party preference known. All registered voters, regardless of party affiliation, can vote on all ballot questions and issues and for all nonpartisan candidates. By going online to dos. myflorida.com/elections and clicking on the "For Voters" drop-down menu, you will be able to:

- Check your voter status and polling place
- View election dates
- Search special election information
- Register to vote in the State of Florida
- Change your name or address
- Replace your defaced, lost or stolen voter registration card
- Register with a political party or change party affiliation
- Update your signature
- Learn alternative ways to vote

Vote-by-Mail

In the event that you are unable or unwilling to make it to your polling location on election day, the state of Florida allows "Vote-by-Mail" ballots. To receive a Vote-by-Mail ballot, you must contact your county Supervisor of Elections.

Make a request to vote by mail through your county Supervisor of Elections website, in writing, in person or by telephone. When making the request, you will be asked for your name, voter address, date of birth and signature if the request is written. Your completed Vote-by-Mail ballot must arrive at the Supervisor of Elections office no later than 7:00 p.m. on Election Day for the vote to be counted.

If you have submitted a request to vote by mail and then later decide to vote at the polls, you must:

- Surrender the Vote-by-Mail ballot at the polls so it may be cancelled.
- If you cannot surrender the Vote-by-Mail ballot (i.e., it is lost), you will be allowed to vote a regular ballot. After

voting in person, the Supervisor of Elections requests that you destroy their original Vote-by-Mail ballot if you come across it in the future.

- A person who requested and returned a Vote-by-Mail ballot to the Supervisor of Elections office may *not* go to the polls to vote. Note: voters who vote more than once in the same election commit a felony and will be turned over to the appropriate authorities for prosecution.

QUESTIONS AND ANSWERS

Voting

Q: How can I find out if I am eligible or registered to vote?

A: If you are uncertain, you can contact your county Supervisor of Elections to ask if you are eligible to vote or to register to vote. You can find contact information for your county Supervisor of Elections by visiting the Florida Department of State, Division of Elections website at dos.myflorida.com/elections and clicking on "Contact your county Supervisor of Elections" in the contact drop-down menu.

Q: How do I register to vote?

A: Information about registering to vote and the Florida voter registration application may be accessed on the Florida Division of Elections website at dos.myflorida.com/elections. Download the form, print it out, complete it and mail it to your county Supervisor of Elections. The form must include an original signature.

Q: Can I send a Vote-by-Mail ballot to an address other than my legal residence?

A: Yes. Your Vote-by-Mail ballot may be sent to your permanent mailing address or a temporary address. If you are sending the ballot to an address that is not on file with the Florida Voter Registration System, the request must be made in writing and signed by the voter.

Q: How do I apply for my Vote-by-Mail ballot and what information is required?

A: A request for a Vote-by-Mail ballot may be made in one of the following ways:

- Online application on your county Supervisor of Elections website
- In writing (e.g., by email, fax, mail) to your Supervisor of Elections
- In person at your Supervisor of Elections office
- By telephone call to your Supervisor of Elections

For example: Written Vote-by-Mail signed requests in Collier County may be mailed to the Collier County Supervisor of Elections, faxed (239-252-2630) or sent as an attachment to an email (MailBallot@colliergov.net).

If you are making the request, the following information is required:

- The name of the voter for whom the ballot is being requested;
- The voter's address;
- The voter's date of birth; and
- The voter's signature (if the request is written).

If an immediate family member or legal guardian is requesting a Vote-by-Mail ballot for you, the following additional information must be provided:

- The requestor's address;
- The requestor's driver license number (if available);
- The requestor's relationship to the voter; and
- The requestor's signature (if the request is written).

" WE LIKE TO SPEND 51 WEEKS OF THE YEAR AT OUR FLORIDA HOLIDAY HOME ... "

My parents didn't want to move to Florida, but they turned sixty and that's the law.
–Jerry Seinfield

CHAPTER 9

CHAPTER 9: FINANCIAL PLANNING FOR FLORIDA RESIDENTS

As you learn more about the many benefits of becoming a Florida resident and declaring the sunny paradise as your domicile, it is probably looking more realistic than ever. The details required to establish Florida residency can seem overwhelming at first but the process is not as daunting as you might think. Once you understand how to prove your intent from the step-by-step guide in Chapter 6, you may have additional concerns like these running through your mind:

- Can I afford to move to Florida?
- Should I sell my northern residence?
- What if I run out of assets?
- Are the savings in state income taxes diminished or eliminated by higher insurance costs?
- Should I take my Social Security benefits at age 62, 66, or 70?
- Do I need state-specific municipal bonds?

- Is long-term care insurance something I need or can afford?
- How do I choose among all the numerous Florida-based financial advisors who claim they want to help me?
- Who can I trust to give me unbiased financial advice?

The above questions are typical of people moving to the Sunshine State. We recommend soon-to-be new Florida residents obtain a comprehensive financial plan developed by a trusted financial planner during the transition.

Florida has an abundance of financial advisors, also known as financial planners and/or consultants, who are eager to sell you financial products and invest your hard-earned money. So, how can you identify, interview and retain a financial planner whose services will meet your objectives? In this chapter, we will define what constitutes a financial plan, describe the types of financial advisors working in Florida, list 10 questions to ask a prospective advisor and introduce you to several planning strategies that may help during your transition.

The Financial Plan

A well-drafted financial plan is one that will bring clarity to your financial clutter and enable you to make appropriate financial decisions to ensure your transition to Florida will be easier. Such a plan involves a specific process so it will provide custom solutions to your individual financial and life objectives.

Six Steps in the Financial Planning Process

1. **Establish and define the client-planner relationship.** In the first step, a financial planner will explain the nature of services to be rendered. The planner will thoroughly articulate his or her responsibilities, along with your responsibilities as the client. He or she will explain and

document fee requirements and any commission structure as well as how and when you will remit payment. You should then both agree on the length of the planning engagement and the scope of services.

It is important to find someone who will not have a conflict of interest. For example, many people think of their investment advisor as their "planner." However, an investment advisor (i.e., stock broker, registered investment advisor, etc.) often has a built-in conflict of interest. For example, if your investment alternatives include real estate or a business venture, the investment advisor has a dilemma—any advice to invest in such alternatives could take money from your market account and his or her pocket in the form of fees and commissions. One option is to work with a fee-only financial planner who specializes in planning, as discussed further below.

2. **Gather client data and determine goals and expectations.** This step is typically called the Discovery Meeting, wherein the financial planner will gather your financial statements, tax returns, trust documents and learn about your family and you. It is during this discovery process that your planner becomes very intimate with your financial information. The planner will also discuss your short-, mid- and long-term financial objectives and needs.

3. **Analyze and evaluate the client financial status.** After Step 2, the financial planner will take all the data gathered from you to organize and analyze the information. This includes entering the information into financial planning software. Some financial planners use a technique called "mind mapping" to help them analyze the data and assist in formulating strategies and tactics. A good financial planner will have a peer review of the data to ensure his or her observations and recommendations are consistent with your objectives.

4. **Present the financial planning recommendations.** The financial planner will then meet with you again to present the recommended financial plan. The plan will have a summary of inputted data and a review of the assumptions, such as projected inflation and investment returns. The planner will then lead you through the plan pointing out potential dangers you need to protect against, opportunities to consider and strengths to build upon. During the meeting, he or she will also cover specific strategies to help you accomplish your objectives.

5. **Implement the financial planning recommendations.** Your planner and you should agree on how to best implement the strategies recommended in the financial plan. This may include collaborating with other professional advisors such as an insurance professional, CPA, estate-planning attorney, etc. If your planner is selling a product for which he or she earns a commission, make sure the compensation is disclosed in writing to you.

Geography: Southwest Florida

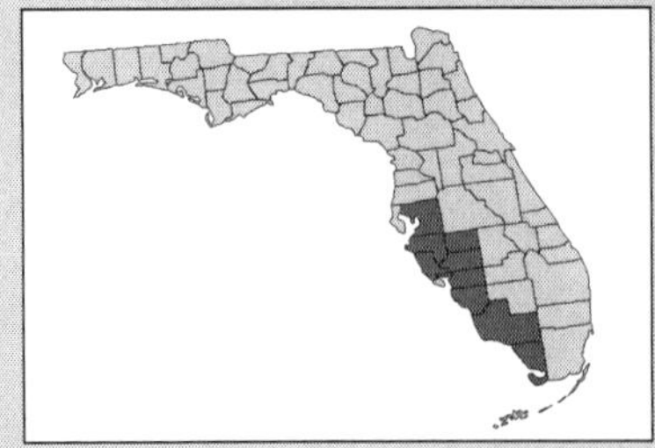

Southwest Florida runs from Tampa south to Everglades City. The major cities in southwest Florida are Tampa, Sarasota, Fort Myers and Naples. On the gulf coast of Florida, superb white sand beaches and resort hotels abound. The beaches in Sarasota and Fort Myers Beach are especially attractive. Sanibel Island and Siesta Key are a mix of the quaint and sophisticated, where visitors can buy from local artists and enjoy fine dining. Inland, Corkscrew Swamp and Six-Mile Cypress Preserve are home to ancient cypress trees. In Tampa, families enjoy Busch Gardens, the Florida Aquarium and Sunken Gardens. Ybor City, the city's Spanish and Cuban district, offers Latin food and culture.

6. **Monitor the financial planning recommendations.** Once the plan is fully implemented, make an agreement with your planner on who is going to monitor your progress. This might include communicating investment performance, future tax planning opportunities and insurance coverage updates.

As noted above, you are best served when you pay for a comprehensive financial plan. Remember, there is no such thing as Santa Claus, the Easter Bunny or a free financial plan. Also, beware of financial advisors who want to invest your money or sell you an insurance product or other investment without first crafting a personalized financial plan.

Facts About Southwest Florida

The name Punta Gorda means "fat point" in Spanish.

The Bailey-Matthews National Shell Museum in Sanibel owns two million shells and claims to be the world's only museum devoted solely to mollusks.

Safety Harbor is the home of the historic Espiritu Santo Springs, named in 1539 by the Spanish explorer Hernando DeSoto. The natural springs have attracted attention worldwide for their curative powers.

Venice is known as the Shark Tooth Capital of the World. Collecting prehistoric sharks' teeth has been a favorite pastime of visitors and residents of the Venice area for years.

Ybor City was once known as the Cigar Capital of the World. With nearly 12,000 tabaqueros (cigar makers) employed in 200 factories, it produced about 700 million cigars a year at the industry's peak.

Understanding Designations

There are over 60 financial advisor designations. How can you distinguish between the credible and the fabricated designations? A good way to learn about a credential is to look it up online and research the qualifications, continuing education requirements and its regulatory board. However, here are some well-known and credible designations to look for in financial advisors:

Certified Financial Planner (CFP®) – A CFP has passed a rigorous test administered by the Certified Financial Planner Board of Standards about the specifics of personal finance. CFPs must also commit to continuing education on financial matters and ethics classes to maintain their designation. The CFP credential is a good sign that a prospective planner will give sound financial advice.

Chartered Financial Consultant (ChFC®) – The ChFC credential was introduced in 1982 as an alternative to the CFP mark. This designation has the same core curriculum as the CFP designation, plus three additional elective courses that focus on various areas of personal financial planning. The biggest difference is that it does not require candidates to pass a comprehensive board exam as with the CFP.

Chartered Financial Analyst (CFA®) – The CFA charter is a qualification for finance and investment professionals, particularly in the fields of investment management and financial analysis of stocks, bonds and their derivative assets. It is widely considered the most difficult test on Wall Street with fewer than 20 percent of successful candidates passing all three exams on their first try.

Chartered Life Underwriter (CLU®) – The CLU is a professional designation for individuals who specialize in life insurance and estate planning. Individuals must complete five core courses, three elective courses and successfully pass all eight two-hour, 100-question examinations to receive the designation.

Certified Public Accountant (CPA) – The CPA designation covers a wide spectrum of accounting and financial analysis services. Lately, increasing numbers of CPAs have chosen to enter the financial planning and advisory arena. Just because a CPA proclaims to be a financial planner does not mean he or she is qualified to render financial advice. Make sure the CPA has specific training in financial planning. For example, look for a CPA who has also earned the CFP or ChFC designation.

The Story of Max Tailwag'er: *A Cautionary Tale*

In 2009, Certified Financial Planner Alan Roth received an unsolicited mailing from The Consumer's Council of America notifying him he had received the "America's Top Financial Planner Award." The return address on the mailing indicated that it originated in Washington, DC, but that was just a mail drop box. Actually, a marketing firm called SLD Industries in Simi Valley, California, sent the award notice. Mr. Roth filled out the award application in the name of his dog, Max, and sent in a check for the required $183. A few weeks later the prestigious plaque arrived naming "Max Tailwag'er" as America's Top Financial Planner. This is a true story reported in Forbes Magazine in 2009 and the incident caused quite a stir. The point? Beware of any financial planner willing to purchase a fabricated "designation" and pass it off as an award.

10 Questions to Ask a Prospective Financial Advisor

1. How do you charge for your services and how much?

If you didn't see this information on the planner's website, ask whether there is an initial planning fee, an hourly fee schedule, whether they charge a percentage for assets under management or whether they make commissions from selling financial products, such as annuities. Of course, it benefits you to know how much the services will cost you but getting answers to these questions will also help you determine whether the planner has an incentive to sell you financial products—products you may not need or want. You might also ask the planner if they accept referral fees from other advisors, such as insurance agents.

2. What is your history and what credentials do you have?

Very few financial planners begin their financial planning careers right out of college. Most seasoned planners have had other careers both in and out of the financial industry. Many of them may have started as insurance agents, trust officers, stockbrokers or tax advisors before entering the financial planning field. These past careers can often act as a benefit to you as this diversified experience makes them well rounded. Regardless of experience, a financial planner's related education and credentials are vitally important. It is a good idea to seek an advisor who is a Certified Financial Planner (CFP®) or Chartered Financial Consultant (ChFC®).

WINGED MIGRATION

If you're feeling a little birdbrained, you are not alone. Visitors flock to Florida to see the Great Florida Birding and Wildlife Trail (GFBWT); over 510 sites throughout the state have been singled out for their outstanding birding opportunities. Florida is home to countless species, from colorful warblers and graceful wading birds to the majestic bald eagle. GFBWT maps and guides make it easy to observe some of Florida's distinctive birds.

Birding is more than just a hobby in Florida. Birders boost local economies when they visit their favorite spots. In 2011, more visitors traveled to Florida to see wildlife than any other state. Tax revenues in 2011 related to all wildlife viewing in Florida amounted to nearly $285 million at the state and local levels.

Source: www.floridabirdingtrail.com

3. What services does your firm provide?

This question will help you determine if the financial planner under consideration is investment-centric or planning-centric. If the planner claims he or she works from a planning-centric perspective but tends to emphasize investment strategies and solutions, you are probably talking to an investment-centric advisor. Many financial planners in practice today are investment-centric. If you want to work with a planning-centric planner who will put your goals and objectives before any potential commission earnings, you need to use extra diligence in vetting prospective financial professionals.

4. What types of clients do you serve best?

This question works well when it comes to identifying a planner's specific area of expertise. For example, you might ask him or her the average age or the generation of most of his or her clients. Chances are, if the planner has some grey hair, he or she probably mostly serves older generations, such as Matures (those born before 1945) and older Baby Boomers. Likewise, his or her presentation style, use of technology and strategies may not appeal to younger clients. Next, ask prospective planners whether they have a niche specialization for their practice. Planners can specialize in numerous areas, including charitable planning, special needs, same sex partners, business exit planning and many others.

5. May I see a sample financial plan?

A good financial planner should be able to not only produce a sample plan but also clearly explain the process from which it was derived. Some financial plans can exceed 50 pages, while others may have only a few pages that give a high-level overview. Ask the financial planner if he or she uses a purchased software package or simply Excel spreadsheets. The use of an Excel spreadsheet requires much more input and analysis of your financial information and, thus, could lead to a more tailored plan.

6. What is your investment approach?

Many financial planners offer investment advisory or

management services. Make sure his or her philosophy and approach are agreeable to you and align with the objectives of your financial plan. Ask the planner if he or she uses active or passive management funds or managers. If the planner picks individual stocks and bonds for client portfolios, ask to see their investment selection process and the names of those on the firm's investment committee.

You might also ask the advisor about the day-to-day activities of the professionals who oversee client portfolios. One common problem with one- or two-person planning firms is that the person who does the planning, marketing, compliance and daily operations is also the same person managing the portfolios. If you like the prospective planner's planning approach but do not wish to use them for investment advisory services, ask if you can hire them just for planning. Most planners typically will not allow you to hire them just for planning services, indicating they are investment-centric.

7. How much and what kind of contact do you have with your clients?

Most planners with a solid process will have an automated system in place for client reviews and communications. Many planners meet with their clients in the first half of the year to review the previous year, update assumptions and re-set the plan in a forward-looking fashion. They then meet with the client at the end of the year for income tax planning, which may include tax loss selling, profit taking, charitable gifts and gifts to family members. Also important is the mode of communication. Increasingly, planners are using the Internet to conduct virtual (video) meetings with clients. Although meeting in person represents the ideal situation, conducting a web-based video meeting can often save time and costs for all involved.

8. Will I be working only with you or with a team?

For planners who work as solo practitioners, this question is easy to answer. But for planners who are part of a group, you should ask if their practice is a "solo" or "ensemble" model. With the solo practice model, each planner has his/her own book of clients and you will have little to no contact with the other planners in the practice. The solo practice represents a more traditional approach and can be very proprietary within the planning practice. An ensemble practice model uses a team approach in which all the professionals in the group serve you. The ensemble practice is becoming increasingly common and often produces the best results for their clients.

9. What makes your client experience unique?

Just about every financial planner will tell you that his approach to planning and investing is unique to him/her. But is it really? For most people, interviews with potential financial planners all begin to sound the same after a while. If the planner's process really is unique, it'll resonate with you and you will walk out of the introductory meeting saying, "WOW!"

Finally, there's one last question you want to ask yourself after meeting with a potential planner:

10. Did he or she ask me questions and seem to understand my values and me as an individual?

To determine your answer, ask yourself these additional discovery questions: Did the prospective planner spend most of the meeting talking about him- or herself? Did he or she ask you questions about your goals and how you feel about wealth? Did he or she speak to you in a manner that put you at ease? Did the planner make you feel you wanted to take a shower as soon as you arrived home after the meeting?

Your relationship with your planner is for the long run, so you want to make sure he or she definitely "gets" you and that your personalities don't clash.

How to Find a Financial Advisor in Florida

Over 300,000 individuals call themselves financial advisors in the United States. And it is rumored that Florida Gulf Coast University generates a higher number of financial planners than any other American university. But how do you find an advisor that is a perfect fit for you? First, you should seriously consider working with a Certified Financial Planner or Chartered Financial Consultant. With that standard in place, here are the three best ways to find a great financial advisor:

Referrals and Recommendations

Ask people you know with backgrounds like yours if they can recommend a planner. If you have kids, ask a colleague who also has children. If possible, you want to find a planner with successful experience advising clients at the same stage of life as you. You may also consider asking an advisor in another profession, such as an estate-planning attorney or CPA, to recommend a financial advisor with whom they have had positive first-hand experiences.

Professional Memberships

Planners who are members of the National Association of Personal Financial Advisors (NAPFA) membership are fee-only, which means their only revenue comes directly from their clients. They accept no commissions at all and pledge to act in their clients' best interests - always. In many respects, NAPFA standards meet or exceed the requirements for obtaining the CFP and ChFC credentials. Their website is www.napfa.org.

The Financial Planning Association (FPA) website (www.plannersearch.org) features an online advisor search engine. Search results will provide you with names and contact information of members of the FPA near you. Unlike the NAPFA search engine, the FPA will provide a cross section of planners who are commission, fee-based and fee-only.

Another website to consider is the American College of Financial Services at www.designationcheck.com. This site can help you:

- Find a financial professional near you who has earned his or her CLU® (Chartered Life Underwriter), ChFC® (Chartered Financial Consultant) or CFP® (Certified Financial Planner) designation;
- Learn more about the credentials financial professionals earn; and
- Explore the questions you should consider when choosing a financial professional.

Transition Planning

In the planning process, we often refer to “transitions.” Transitions are often the result of life changing events—new job, marriage, retirement, etc. If you are contemplating changing your domicile to Florida, you are in transition. Thus, it is important for you to take the time to plan. The best way to plan is to find a financial planner who can earn your trust and help you succeed in achieving your goals.

Success and Sunshine - A Trusted Financial Planner to Enhance Both

Your association with a financial planner can and should develop into a long-term, trusting relationship. Take your time and do your homework when choosing an advisor who will act as your fiduciary and guide you through life’s financial complexities. When you’ve worked with an advisor over a long period of time, it gives both of you a feeling of accomplishment as you track your progress toward meeting short- and long-term financial and lifestyle goals. The right financial planner can make your Florida days even sunnier than you ever imagined.

"I'D LIKE YOU TO ENDORSE MY LIFESTYLE."

PART 3

THE FLORIDA LIFESTYLE

The Florida lifestyle is a celebration of leisure, culture, recreation and entertainment. For many Floridians, home is where there is plenty of sand between the toes and lots of tees between the greens.

But that's not all. From gulfside fishing villages that open and close with the tides to vibrant cities filled with cosmopolitan flair, Florida provides plenty of variety for anyone in search of the good life.

Home sales in Florida continue to rise as buyers continue to relocate in search of a sound investment and a desirable home. And waiting for them are world-class amenities, spectacular beaches, outstanding cultural centers, state-of-the-art medical facilities, quality schools and universities, fine dining, abundant shopping and a wealth of recreational opportunities that promise a lifestyle beyond compare in a location beyond all expectations.

"THE MEANING OF LIFE IS LOCATION, LOCATION, LOCATION."

There is nothing like staying at home for real comfort.
– Jane Austen

CHAPTER 10

PURCHASING A HOME IN FLORIDA

If you are contemplating purchasing a Florida residence, go to fl.living.net, a consumer website by Florida Realtors® that allows you to easily search active listings within any county in Florida. Alternately, you can also pick up a local Florida newspaper, especially the Sunday edition, and drive around looking at property in the area where you have decided you want to live. After you get serious about home ownership, your next best move is to contact a qualified REALTOR® who specializes in residential real estate.

Any person who is properly licensed in Florida can sell Florida real estate. However, the term "Realtor" refers to someone who also subscribes to the strict Code of Ethics of the National Association of REALTORS® and has access to the Realtor Multiple Listing Service (MLS). The MLS (www.mls.com) provides current and historical information on properties that have been placed on the market by all Realtors in the area covered by the local board of Realtors. In addition to the strict code of ethics and the MLS, there are continuing educational requirements that separate a Realtor from a salesperson who is simply licensed under an established Florida real estate broker.

The National Association of REALTORS®, in conjunction with local boards of Realtors, offers educational courses to their members that lead to various designations, such as Certified Residential Specialist (CRS) and Graduate Realtors Institute (GRI). These designations plus others, if earned, show a Realtor's commitment to his or her profession as well as an added degree of knowledge about the Realtor's chosen specialty.

One of the biggest advantages of working with a qualified Florida Realtor is their knowledge of the local area, including proximity to schools, shopping, recreation and new planned developments. In addition, the Realtor MLS can provide substantial information on properties that are on the market in the area you have selected and, thereby, save you a great deal of time and energy. Most MLS systems are computerized, so you or your Realtor will be able to access a large amount of information, usually including pictures, through the Internet.

Representation

It is important to know that a Florida Realtor can arrange to represent either the seller or the buyer (buyer's broker) as a single agent or may enter into a brokerage relationship as a transaction broker. A Realtor may not operate as a dual agent, which means he or she can not represent, as a fiduciary, both a prospective buyer and a prospective seller in a real estate transaction, whether it is disclosed or not.

Under the law in Florida, it is presumed that all licensees are operating as transaction brokers unless a single agent or no brokerage relationship is established, in writing, with a prospective customer.

Transaction Broker: A transaction broker provides a limited form of representation to a buyer, a seller or both in a real estate transaction but does not represent either in a fiduciary capacity or as a single agent. The duties of the Realtor in this limited form of representation include the following:

- Dealing honestly and fairly;

- Accounting for all funds;
- Using skill, care and diligence in the transaction;
- Disclosing all known facts that materially affect the value of residential real property and are not readily observable to the buyer;
- Presenting all offers and counteroffers in a timely manner, unless a party has previously directed the licensee otherwise in writing;
- Limited confidentiality, unless waived in writing by a party. This limited confidentiality will prevent disclosure regarding the following: 1.) that the seller will accept a price less than the asking or listed price, 2.) that the buyer will pay a price greater than the price submitted in a written offer, 3.) of the motivation of any party for selling or buying property, 4.) that a seller or buyer will agree to financing terms other than those offered or 5.) of any other information requested by a party to remain confidential; and
- Any additional duties that are mutually agreed to with a party.

Limited representation means that a buyer or seller is not responsible for the acts of the real estate professional. Additionally, the parties to a real estate transaction are giving up their rights to the undivided loyalty of the licensee. This aspect of limited representation allows a Realtor to facilitate a real estate transaction by assisting both the buyer and seller but a Realtor will not work to represent one party to the detriment of the other party when acting as a transaction broker to both parties.

Single Agent: The duties of a Florida Realtor who is engaged by a buyer or seller as a single agent include the following:

- Dealing honestly and fairly;
- Loyalty;

- Confidentiality;
- Obedience;
- Full disclosure;
- Accounting for all funds;
- Skill, care and diligence in the transaction;
- Presenting all offers and counteroffers in a timely manner, unless a party has previously directed the licensee otherwise in writing; and
- Disclosing all known facts that materially affect the value of residential real property and are not readily observable.

The above duties by a single agent must be fully described and disclosed in writing to a buyer or seller either as a separate and distinct disclosure document or included as part of another document such as a listing agreement or other agreement for representation. The disclosure must be made before, or at the time of, entering into a listing agreement or an agreement for representation or before the showing of property, whichever occurs first.

Transition: A single agent relationship in a residential sale may be changed to a transaction broker relationship at any time during the relationship between an agent and principal, provided the agent first obtains the principal's written consent to the change in their relationship. This disclosure must be in writing to you, as the principal, either as a separate and distinct document or included as part of other documents such as a listing agreement or other agreements for representation and include the above listed duties relating to the type of relationship being sought. The term "residential sale" means the sale of improved residential property of four units or fewer, the sale of unimproved residential property intended for use of four units or fewer or the sale of agricultural property of 10 acres or fewer.

No Brokerage Relationship: In a Florida real estate transaction, a licensee who has no brokerage relationship with a potential seller or buyer has the following duties under law:

- Dealing honestly and fairly;
- Disclosing all known facts that materially affect the value of the residential real property which are not readily observable to the buyer; and
- Accounting for all funds entrusted to the licensee.

Duties of a licensee who has no brokerage relationship with a buyer or seller must be fully described, as noted above, and disclosed in writing to the buyer or seller. The disclosure must be made before the showing of property.

Limitations: The real estate disclosure requirements above do not apply when a licensee knows that the potential seller or buyer is represented by a single agent or a transaction broker or when an owner is selling new residential units built by the owner and the circumstances or setting should reasonably inform the potential buyer that the owner's employee or single agent is acting on behalf of the owner.

Confirm Your Representation: It is important to confirm your relationship with the real estate professional you select—at your first meeting. Most real estate agents will act as transactional agents as many brokers will not permit a single agent relationship. Under Florida law, Realtors operate as transaction brokers; however, you may elect to establish a single agent relationship and have the Realtor represent you as a buyer or as a seller. This is done in a written disclosure agreement making it clear exactly who the Realtor agrees to represent in a fiduciary capacity.

Some Realtors specialize in representing buyers via a signed single agent relationship agreement and frequently call themselves a "buyer's broker." This allows them to attempt to get the most favorable deal for you, as a home buyer. In this arrangement, you would typically agree to pay the Realtor to find the "right" property at the lowest possible price.

Regardless of which relationship you elect to establish, you will benefit from the knowledge, integrity and professionalism when working with a Realtor.

Negotiating

After locating the home of your choice, the next step is to have your Realtor negotiate an agreement, in writing, with the seller of the property. The local board of Realtors supplies Realtors with a standard sales agreement, which you can use to make an offer to a seller. These contracts are carefully designed to cover most of the important items necessary for consideration when purchasing and selling a parcel of real estate. However, it may be wise to employ a Florida real estate attorney to ensure that all the bases have been covered and your interests are fully protected. You may want to hire a civil engineer or other qualified property inspector to ensure that the home meets all the applicable building codes and does not have any major defects.

One option is to make an offer that is subject to review by your Florida attorney, so that the terms will not be final until your attorney has reviewed the contract and made any changes necessary to protect your best interests.

In a typical real estate transaction, the buyer provides a deposit with an offer to purchase to illustrate that the offer is made in "earnest." There is no standard amount for a deposit but five to ten percent of the purchase price is common. Often the amount is small (e.g., one percent) until the offer is accepted.

Financing

Most standard real estate sales contracts include a section that calls for the agreement to be contingent upon the purchaser's success in obtaining financing. Unless you do not need to finance your purchase, you should also seek to make your transaction contingent on your ability to secure financing for your purchase.

Completing the sales contract correctly and ensuring the transaction is contingent on financing is crucial to ensure you do not end up losing any deposits that you have made in connection with the transaction. You should also be certain to give your mortgage lender enough time to complete the approval process, which usually includes an appraisal and a survey.

There are numerous sources in Florida for obtaining real estate loans, including banks, mortgage companies, mortgage brokers and private lenders. It is generally a good idea to deal with a lender that offers a variety of financing choices (such as conventional fixed-rate mortgages, adjustable-rate mortgages and interest-only mortgages) and has a good track record of lending in the county where the property you are purchasing is located. You want to make sure the lender you choose will be able to make a firm commitment to provide the funds in a specified period of time and stick to the rate quoted to you.

Transfer of Title from an Estate

If the property is passing from an estate, legal and tax issues can easily foul up the timing of the sale and/or closing. The Internal Revenue Service (IRS) and Florida Department of Revenue (DOR) have automatic tax liens for estate taxes and other tax liabilities that accrued before the death of a taxpayer and remain unpaid on all properties owned by a decedent at the time of death. The tax liens must be cleared to convey clear title to the new owner (either by sale or by inheritance). Depending on the size of the decedent-owner's taxable estate, the method and timing of the clearance of the liens will be different. You should consult a legal adviser who is competent in these matters if you plan to purchase a home from a Florida estate.

Title Insurance and Surveys

As a real estate purchaser, to ensure that you are getting proper title—free from all encumbrances—from the seller, have your attorney examine the title and boundary survey of the property and consider purchasing title insurance to protect your interest against serious financial loss due to a defect in the title to the property. The one-time title insurance premium, which is a modest amount in relationship to the value of the property, provides you, as a buyer, with protection that is backed by the reserves and solvency of the Title Underwriter. A title insurance policy will cover both claims arising out of title problems that could have been discovered in the public records and those so-called "non-record" defects that could not be discovered in the record even with the most complete title search.

A title insurance policy will not only protect the insured owner but also that person's heirs for as long as they hold title to the property and even after they sell by warranty deed. The underwriter will not only satisfy any valid claim made against the insured's title but it will pay for the costs and legal expenses of defending against a title claim.

Once title insurance is purchased, the average property owner will not, typically, have to think about it again. When the owner sells his property, he may be asked to furnish his title policy to serve as "evidence of title" for his buyer. At that time, minor title problems may also be resolved with indemnifications furnished by his title insurer to the buyer. Outright title challenges rarely occur. However, when they do, they can be disastrous, both in terms of legal expenses and loss of equity. If you are obtaining financing, the mortgage lender will require title insurance, protecting the lender, in the amount of the mortgage.

Although the seller is often required to furnish evidence of title (usually in the form of the seller's title insurance or an abstract of title, which is a condensed history taken from the public records, etc., that can be recertified to the date of the closing of the sale), the buyer normally pays the premium for the new title insurance, including the mortgage title policy. However, in a real estate transaction, everything is negotiable, including who pays for the title insurance and amounts paid to real estate professionals for their services.

A survey helps determine and confirm the question of the marketability of the real estate. The surveyor determines whether the improvements (house, garage, outbuildings, etc.) are within the property borders, whether there are any encroachments on the property by neighbors and the extent to which any easements on the property may affect legal title.

Importance of Having Legal Representation

The purchase of real property in Florida can often be a life-changing and emotional event. Title companies and Realtors are not legally permitted to provide you with any legal advice or guidance. A title company only prepares the closing documents in conjunction with the transaction and issues title insurance. Attorneys represent your best interest from contract to close and endeavor to solve any problems that arise throughout the closing process. This reason alone sets attorneys apart and makes it vital that you have an attorney represent you. The importance of wholly protecting your real estate investment cannot be overstated.

Closing

The closing is usually scheduled to take place after all the contingencies, such as inspections, have been completed. The closing can be done at the office of the seller's attorney but is often conducted at the office of the closing agency furnishing the title insurance or the office of the mortgage lender, if any is involved. In Florida, it is not necessary to have all the parties appear at the closing. In fact, it is not unusual for the buyer to appear without the seller present, as the deed and other papers are often signed in advance by the seller and held in escrow until the buyer has signed and paid the funds for purchase.

The Realtor or the lender should provide a copy of the closing statement—which will list the charges and credits pertaining to the purchase and sale of the real estate—before the closing. All closing agents typically will require a wire transfer of the purchase price plus other closing costs made payable to the trust account of the closing agent at closing. After all the closing papers are signed, including the closing statement, deed and any mortgages, the closing agent will disburse the proceeds according to the closing statement and will be responsible for recording the deed in the Recording Department office in the county where the property is located.

Allocating Closing Costs

The costs associated with the purchase of real estate vary, depending on the Florida county in which you are buying. However, in a typical sale in Florida, costs are shared between the buyer and seller, as detailed on the next page.

The **buyer's costs** include the following:

- Deposits
- Title insurance
- Documentary stamps on the note
- Intangible tax on the mortgage
- Inspection fees
- Appraisal
- Survey fee
- Loan fees
- Prepaid interest
- Mortgage insurance
- Hazard insurance
- Condominium/ homeowner association membership approval recording fee
- Condominium/ homeowner association membership transfer fee
- Recording fees per the title insurance commitment

The **seller's costs** include the following:

- Loan payoff
- Real estate broker's commission
- Documentary stamps on the deed of transfer
- Prorated real estate taxes
- Title search fee
- Lien search fee
- Title evidence
- Preparation of transfer documents (deed, bill of sale, etc.)
- Balance due on any government liens or special assessments

Other closing costs that may apply include prorated items and credits for the following:

- Ad valorem and non-ad valorem real and personal property taxes
- Interest on any assumable indebtedness
- Rents and security deposits
- Condominium/homeowner association assessments
- County waste assessments
- Utility services
- Appliance service contracts to be assumed by the buyer
- A current Uniform Commercial Code (UCC) encumbrance search
- Preparation of a purchase-money mortgage note and documentary stamps and recording fees relating to it

" THE FIRST THING YOU NEED TO DO IS LOSE 40 POUNDS OF THAT BABY BOOMER FAT. "

Be careful about reading health books.
You may die of a misprint.
–Mark Twain

CHAPTER 11

FLORIDA INSURANCE AND HEALTH CARE OPTIONS

When you become a Florida resident, you should focus on protecting your future by reviewing your insurance coverage. At a minimum, you should check on the benefits of purchasing protection for your home and business. Further, the right type of health maintenance program and insurance coverage will help keep you going strong so you can continue enjoying the benefits of being a Florida resident.

Homeowner's Insurance

Although Florida law does not require it, homeowner's insurance can help you in the event of a loss of your home and/or personal property. There are four basic insurance types:

Fire: Fire insurance protects you in the event of a loss from fire and smoke.

Flood: Flood insurance can be particularly important especially if your home is located in a flood zone.

Wind: Windstorm coverage protects you in the event of damage to your home and/or personal property from tornadoes, hurricanes and wind.

Liability: Virtually all homeowners' policies provide liability coverage, which pays for non-automobile-related injuries to other persons or their property.

Some cities and counties require you to have liability insurance if you have a swimming pool or own certain pets. In most cases, if you have a mortgage, the lender will typically require all four of the above insurance coverage types. Some developers and subdivisions may also require you to maintain liability insurance on your home.

Condominium Owner's Insurance

Under Florida law, condominium associations must provide a minimum standard of insurance coverage. The association policy must cover all structures and other common property. You should take the time to examine your association's policy to learn what it covers. The premium for the association policy is typically included in the periodic condominium maintenance fee each homeowner is required to pay.

Condominium Interior Insurance

For the loss protection on that portion of the structure not covered by the association policy, such as your interior wallpaper, trim, built-in book cases, cabinets, fixtures, carpeting, interior liability, etc. and for personal property, you will want to consider purchasing condominium interior insurance. Interior policies are separate from the association policy and the additional cost is your responsibility and is not included in your condominium maintenance fees.

Property Insurance for High-Risk Areas

In 2002, the Florida legislature passed a law combining the former Florida Residential Property and Casualty Joint Underwriting Association (FRPCJUA) and the Florida Windstorm Underwriting Association (FWUA). The result was the creation of Citizens Property Insurance Corporation (Citizens). This new nonprofit, tax-exempt, government entity operates with the mission to efficiently and effectively provide insurance to and serve the needs of Florida homeowners in high-risk areas as well as to those who cannot find coverage in the private insurance market.

For more information, contact Citizens Property Insurance Corporation at their Customer Care department by telephone at (888) 685-1555 or online at www.citizensfla.com.

You can obtain general information regarding homeowner's insurance from the Florida Office of Insurance Regulation online at www.floir.com.

Umbrella Policy for Extended Liability Coverage

To add a layer of protection for personal liability against injuries to other persons or property, you should consider purchasing an umbrella policy, which typically increases the liability limits of your homeowner's or condominium insurance by an additional amount (e.g., $2 million). Umbrella policies are usually reasonably priced and require you to have base coverage, sometimes with the same insurer, on your Florida home and/or other investment property.

Health Care Programs and Services

In the past, Florida has suffered from a reputation as being "God's waiting room." While it is true that many people move to Florida after retirement, Florida boasts a remarkable medical industry with both cutting edge technology and competitive pricing. It is home to satellite facilities for the Mayo Clinic and Cleveland

A River of Grass

One of Florida's most recognized features is the Everglades, often called the "river of grass." Historically, the Everglades consisted of a vast network of interconnected wetlands, covering about 8.9 million acres from Orange County to Florida Bay.

Author Marjory Stoneman Douglas played a major role in bringing outside recognition and appreciation to the Everglades. Her classic 1947 book, *The Everglades: River of Grass*, helped win support for curbing development and draining projects that threatened this unique Florida feature. During the 1950s, sweeping drainage projects diverted or eradicated much of the historic Everglades, affecting Florida's natural water cycle and harming wildlife. The 1994 Everglades Forever Act requires that the Everglades' natural flow be restored and water quality be improved for the benefit of all Florida.

Source: Florida Department of Environmental Protection.

Reprinted with permission of www.Bigstock.com

Clinic as well as exceptional specialty programs that are making medical history in the areas of fertility, gerontology, heart research and pharmacology. Check online at www.Floridahealth.gov.

When asked, most Florida health care providers agree that prevention is the key to success when it comes to public health. Staying informed as a patient involves finding out more about your medical status, your medical conditions, the medical procedures or treatments available and learning how to get coverage for the appropriate treatment and care.

Health Care Assistance

Below are health care programs and assistance available for Florida residents who meet certain income requirements. These programs and services may help if you do not have insurance or if your insurance does not adequately cover your needs.

Community Health Centers

Community health centers are federally funded to provide health care in medically underserved areas. To find out if there is a health center in your area and to view a list of services, visit the U.S. Department of Health Resources and Services Administration's website at www.hrsa.gov.

County Health Departments

Florida county health departments provide some medical services for low cost or no fee depending upon income. To find an office in your area and the programs and services available, visit www.floridahealth.gov and search "Find a county health department."

Benefits for People with Disabilities

The Social Security Administration (SSA) offers two types of disability benefits: Social Security Disability Insurance (SSDI) and Supplemental Security Income (SSI). These two programs are the largest of several Federal programs to provide assistance to people with disabilities who meet certain medical criteria. For a comprehensive list of disability-related government resources, visit www.ssa.gov/disability.

Florida Department of Elder Affairs

Florida Department of Elder Affairs (DOEA) offers several community-based programs to assist elders in their homes. Information can be obtained online at elderaffairs.state.fl.us or call the Elder Help Line toll-free at (800) 963-5337.

National Council on Aging

If you are fifty-five years of age or over, the National Council on Aging has a website at www.benefitscheckup.org with referrals to many programs offering assistance with the cost of medications. It includes information on state-funded programs, state Medicaid programs and company-sponsored patient assistance programs. You can complete a brief questionnaire online and obtain a report on all the programs you might be eligible for and instructions on how to enroll in them.

Medicare

Medicare is a federal health insurance program for people who are age sixty-five or older, for disabled persons or for those with end-stage kidney disease. There are four major parts to the Medicare program:

Part A: Hospital Insurance

Part B: Medical Expense Insurance

Part C: Medicare Advantage (Medicare + Choice)

Part D: Prescription Drug Program

Financing for the Medicare program comes from three sources: government revenue, premiums from Medicare beneficiaries and Medicare taxes paid by most working persons and employers.

You can find information on Medicare, Medicare HMOs, Medicare Part D Prescription Drug Program and Medicare supplemental insurance online at www.medicare.gov or by calling toll-free (800) 633-4227.

Medicaid

Medicaid provides access to health care for low-income individuals who qualify. Applications for Medicaid and other services are taken at a local office of the Florida Department of Children and Families (DCF); get more information online at www.myFLfamilies.com or by phone at (866) 762-2237.

The Agency for Health Care Administration, at (888) 419-3456, provides information on Medicaid covered services. For a list of locations and phone numbers of AHCA Medicaid area offices, call the Florida Medicaid Program at (800) 289-7799.

SHINE Program

Serving Health Insurance Needs of Elders (SHINE) is a free, volunteer-based health insurance counseling program for seniors administered by the Florida Department of Elder Affairs and your local Area Agency on Aging. The program assists seniors in making informed health care decisions regarding Medicare, Medicaid and health insurance by providing counseling to those who need it. Information on Medicare HMO coverage in Florida, as well as other programs and services, can be obtained at www.floridashine.org or by calling (800) 96-ELDER (800-963-5337).

Medicare Part D Prescription Drug Benefit

Medicare Part D is a type of insurance to help people with Medicare pay for prescription drugs. As of January 1, 2006, the Medicare Part D Prescription Drug benefit is provided through Medicare-approved private health plans. If you receive health coverage through Medicare and the Florida Medicaid program, your prescription drugs are covered under the Medicare Part D benefit. If you have Medicare coverage but not Medicaid, you can enroll in a Medicare Part D drug plan but you are not required to do so.

You should compare the various drug plans, including Medicare Part D, before you choose one to see which will cover the prescription medicines you take, how much coverage they offer, which pharmacies you can use with each plan, the cost of deductibles, copayments and the monthly premium.

Florida residents enrolled in Medicare Part A (hospital insurance) and/or Part B (medical insurance) are eligible for the prescription drug coverage (Part D). Additionally, individuals eligible for both Medicare and Medicaid benefits (dual eligible) may also enroll in the Part D program.

Under the Medicare Part D program, a participant's out-of-pocket costs for covered medications in 2017, depending upon the Medicare Plan you select, will include:

- **Monthly Premium** – \$35 to \$37 paid by the Medicare Beneficiary
- **Annual Deductible** – \$400 paid by the Medicare Beneficiary
- **Cost of Prescriptions** – \$401 to \$3,700 with 25% paid by the Medicare Beneficiary and 75% paid by Medicare
- **Cost of Prescriptions** – \$3,701 to \$7,425 (The "Donut Hole")

- **100% Paid by the Medicare Beneficiary** – 0% paid by Medicare
- **More than $4,950 annual out-of-pocket threshold** – If you have spent $4,950 on Medicare Part D drugs (not including monthly Medicare plan premiums), you will exit the Donut Hole and enter the **Catastrophic Coverage** phase where the Medicare Beneficiary pays the greater of either 5% of the prescription drug costs or $3.30 for generic prescription drugs and $8.25 for brand-name prescription drugs. Medicare Part D pays the lesser of 95% of the prescription drug costs or the balance of the prescription drug costs.

Available plans may vary from these guidelines (see: Medicare Part D Plan Overview for Florida by visiting www.medicarehelp.org and selecting "Medicare Part-D Plans" from the Medicare dropdown menu).

You can find more information and help with enrollment by calling Medicare's toll-free number (800) 633-4227 or by visiting www.medicare.gov.

SHINE also has trained volunteers who can assist you with questions about the Medicare Part D Prescription Drug benefit.

Alternative Prescription Drug Assistance Programs

Florida residents, including children, families and senior citizens, also have various alternative programs to assist them in covering the cost of prescription drugs. Plans for senior citizens are available to individuals with limited incomes and who have both Medicare and Medicaid benefits or Social Security Income (SSI) assistance. A complete list of service providers is available at www.floridashine.org or call (800) 963-5337. It is advisable that individuals residing part of the year in Florida consider a plan that provides national coverage.

The state of Florida also provides a discount drug card for all residents through the Florida Discount Drug Card Program without restriction and is accepted at over 60,000 pharmacies nationwide. You may download the Florida discount card at www.floridadiscountdrugcard.com or request a card be sent to you by calling (866) 341-8894.

Working with the Agency for Health Care Administration, Florida's Office of the Attorney General also provides a dedicated website to help consumers shop for the lowest prescription price in their area. You can search by county and drug name at www.myfloridarx.com.

Florida KidCare Program

KidCare is a Florida health insurance program for children, which provides medical coverage at low or no cost, depending on family income. Information may be obtained at www.floridakidcare.org or by calling toll-free at (888) 540-5437.

County Resources

Health care and prescription assistance can also be found through many local health departments and non-profit programs. For example, in Collier County, the Neighborhood Health Clinic coordinates and delivers health care for low-income working residents. Contact your county medical society to see if it can refer you to a similar local resource.

Health Maintenance Organizations

Health Maintenance Organizations (HMOs) are a type of health insurance plan regulated by the Agency for Health Care Administration (AHCA) and the Department of Financial Services. To find out more, visit www.ahca.myflorida.com.

The Florida HMO Report includes a list of specific HMOs serving different areas of Florida, a summary of the various HMO services and the results of a member satisfaction survey. It is available at www.floridahealthfinder.gov under the health plans tab or you can order a copy by calling toll-free at (888) 419-3456.

Florida Nursing Home Guide

The Nursing Home Guide provides advice for choosing a Florida nursing home, including which insurance payments are accepted by which nursing homes. It also has a rating system using common criteria to assess nursing home quality. Instructions on how to interpret, use and download the guide are available at www.floridahealthfinder.gov under the health plans tab or order it by calling (888) 419-3456.

Direct Care Providers and Concierge Medicine

Due to a rise in premiums and a reduction in covered conditions, many residents in Florida are going outside the insurance arena and choosing to pay health care providers directly—to obtain a higher level of service, such as house calls, physician access 24/7, no waiting room time, etc. This type of service is called "concierge" medicine.

An example of one Florida health care provider with a concierge practice and high level of service is Dr. Richard M. Kravis in Collier County (www.kravismd.com). His concierge practice offers extraordinary services compared to many typical primary care physicians, including home visits, comprehensive annual physical examinations, health assessment and lifestyle planning, wellness recommendations and preventative education.

Health Guides for Families and Individuals

Several guides are available from the Agency for Health Care

Administration as a reference to assist consumers in evaluating their health care options in Florida. View and download them at www.floridahealthfinder.gov/index.html.

Long-Term Care Insurance

Floridians are living longer and healthier lives, thanks to Florida's rejuvenating climate, better medical care, better diet and safer living and working environments. However, no one is immune from the effects of aging, which often result in reduced mental or physical ability. You or a loved one could need long-term care (LTC) services in your home or elsewhere because of aging, a disabling disease or a serious accident—situations that could happen to anyone.

Having family or friends act as caregivers may not always be a realistic option. The alternative is professional LTC services, which may be provided by a health care professional, such as a nurse, a home health aide or other personal care providers on a part-time or full-time basis. The services can be provided in a setting such as your own home, an assisted living facility, an adult day care center or a nursing home.

According to the U.S. Department of Health and Human Services, seven out of ten people will need some form of long-term care during their lives (see: www.longtermcare.gov). With an

Leading Causes for LTC	Length of Care
Alzheimer's disease	96 months
Cancer	36 months
Cardiac Conditions	16 months
Diabetes	48 months
Pulmonary Conditions	36 months
Stroke	21 months

average stay in a nursing home of approximately 2.2 years for men and 2.7 years for women, the cost can be staggering. Even if your plan is to be cared for at home, that period of care can be lengthy and the associated costs prohibitive.

Many Florida seniors are shocked when they realize that Medicare will not fully cover their health care costs after retirement, particularly long-term care costs. The reality is that Medicare only covers nursing home costs for a very short period. At best, Medicare will pay for all or part of the first one hundred days of care and only if it follows a hospital stay to recuperate from an acute illness or injury. Anyone with even a passing experience with Alzheimer's disease, stroke, Parkinson's disease or simply elder frailty can appreciate the severity and financial devastation of these all too common life events. The box on page 208 displays the statistics on the length of care needed for major illnesses frequently requiring long-term care. To get an idea of the cost, according to AARP (www.aarp.org), the average rate in 2017 for a private room in a Naples, Florida, nursing home was $329 per day. At a compounded annual inflation rate of 5 percent, the LTC costs for that same private room in 2025 would be a little over $177,420 per year.

Even the cost of in-home care can be substantial. The average hourly cost for a home care aide worker in 2017 was approximately $21 per hour and, when the need is great, such as in the case of Alzheimer's disease, the overall costs of home care can mount up quickly and cause significant financial stress. In fact, failure to plan for LTC is the primary cause of poverty among older Americans. The best way to be prepared for the cost of LTC is to purchase LTC insurance.

When purchasing LTC insurance, you should consider four basic components in your decision:

- Benefit amount: The maximum fixed-dollar amount that a policy will pay each day.
- Inflation adjustment: The increase in the benefit amount to cover the effect of inflation.

- Benefit period: The length of time an LTC policy will pay for covered services (e.g., two years to unlimited time).
- Elimination period: The number of days that you pay for covered services before the policy pays (e.g., 30-, 60-, 90-, 120- or 365-day period).

To learn more about your choices, contact an LTC agent who is licensed to do business in Florida.

When shopping for an appropriate long-term care insurance policy, financial strength is a key consideration. There are several established insurer rating services, such as A.M. Best Company (www.ambest.com), Fitch, Inc. (www.fitchratings.com), Moody's Investor Service, Inc. (www.moodys.com), Standard & Poor's Insurance Rating Services (standardandpoors.com) and Weiss Research, Inc. (www.weissinc.com). Visit them online or go to your local Florida public library.

In addition to ratings, the reputation of an insurer is also important. You can contact the Florida Insurance Commissioner regarding an insurance company's status and any complaints from policyholders. Also, you may obtain a copy of "A Shopper's Guide to Long-Term Care Insurance" from the National Association of Insurance Commissioners online at www.naic.org or by phone at (816) 783-8300.

If you are contemplating purchasing health insurance, you should verify whether the company is authorized to do business in Florida. In most cases, the benefits of authorized Florida insurers are guaranteed through the Florida Insurance Guarantee Association (FIGA) at www.figafacts.com and the Florida Life and Health Insurance Guaranty Association (FLHIGA) at www.flahiga.org which provide the following:

- FIGA pays the claims of property and casualty authorized insurers if the company becomes insolvent and cannot pay.

- FLHIGA pays the claims of life and health authorized insurers if the company becomes insolvent and cannot pay.

If you purchase insurance from a company that is not authorized to do business in Florida, you run the risk of not having the protections listed previously.

When selecting an agent to help you purchase the correct insurance, you should choose one who is licensed to sell insurance in Florida as well as an agent you feel comfortable with who will be available to answer your questions, handle your policy and provide on-going service.

Health Information Resources

Find any type of health care facility in Florida—including hospitals, home health agencies, nursing homes, assisted living facilities, skilled nursing centers and hospices—at florida-healthfinder.gov. The Florida Hospital Association also lists hospitals and health systems throughout Florida at www.fha.org. There are many publications and other resources available to help you with information on health insurance issues, including the American Association of Retired Persons (AARP), which has information on health insurance for seniors at www.aarp.org/health/medicare-insurance.

Additional information on health insurance companies and consumer insurance guides may be obtained from any of the following sources:

- Florida Department of Financial Services, Consumer helpline, (800) 342-2762
- Office of Insurance Regulation, www.floir.com
- Florida Department of Financial Services Consumer Guides, www.myfloridacfo.com/division/consumers or (877-693-5236)

"It's not your traditional report. I've done it in the form of a YouTube video.

Education is the kindling of a flame,
not the filling of a vessel.
–Socrates

CHAPTER 12

FLORIDA EDUCATION

Educational opportunities abound throughout Florida. Whether you are 3, 33 or 83, there are programs available to further your knowledge, creativity and enjoyment of this great state. From prekindergarten to college to adult education, Floridians have endless opportunities to keep busy, keep abreast and to continue learning and growing.

Early Years

In Florida, before a child enters kindergarten, each school is required to administer a kindergarten readiness screening. In 2005, the Florida Voluntary Prekindergarten (VPK) legislation was signed into law by then-Governor Jeb Bush. This law created a program to prepare Florida four-year-olds for kindergarten and to build a strong foundation for their continued educational success. The program is free (at participating schools) and participation is voluntary. For more information on VPK and early learning/prekindergarten, visit www.vpkhelp.org.

Primary and Secondary Education

In Florida, K-12 students and parents are afforded the right to education choice. Whether parents live in a school district that offers school choice, are changing residences or have a child entering kindergarten, choosing a school is a complex decision that includes the characteristics of the child, family and schools. These choices include public school, independent/private school, home education and private tutoring. To learn more about the different types of educational choices in Florida, go to www.floridaschoolchoice.org.

Public K-12 schools in Florida are individually ranked based on data from the Florida Comprehensive Assessment Test (FCAT) provided by the Florida Department of Education. You can search school rankings at www.greatschools.org/florida.

The No Child Left Behind (NCLB) law means states and school districts must provide "report cards" for parents. The information is tailored for parents, telling them about the quality of education at their child's school. Written in an easy-to-read format, these report cards ensure that parents and taxpayers know which schools are achieving

Geography: The Florida Panhandle

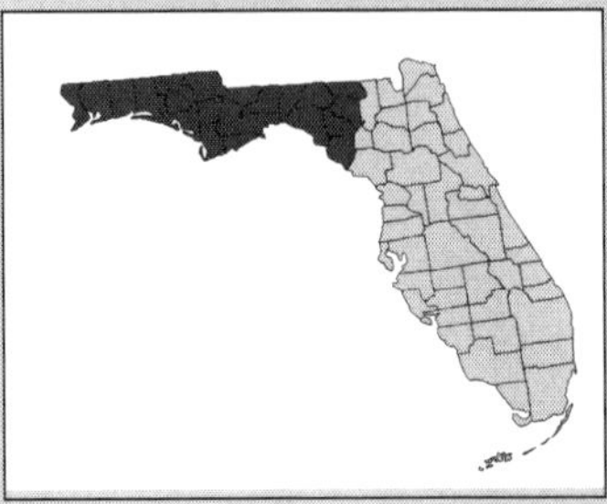

The boundaries of the Florida Panhandle run from Florida's western border with Alabama east to Lake City. Major cities in the Panhandle include Pensacola, Tallahassee, Apalachicola and Fort Walton Beach. Colorful fishing towns line the coast which is also a major attraction for surfers. Tallahassee is the state capital and is home to Florida State University. Hunting, fishing and hiking opportunities abound in vast forests and, for a change of pace, visit Florida Caverns State Park, one of the only dry caves in Florida.

and how. The report cards include student achievement data broken out by race, ethnicity, gender, English language proficiency, as well as data on whether the students are immigrants or have disabilities and whether they are disadvantaged. States and school districts must also provide parents and children in struggling schools timely notification of the public school choice and supplemental services options that may be available.

Post-Secondary Education

Eleven public universities and a liberal arts college comprise the State University System of Florida. In addition, the Florida College System includes 28 public community colleges and state colleges. Florida also has many private universities, some of which comprise the Independent Colleges and Universities of Florida.

Facts About The Florida Panhandle

DeFuniak Springs is home to one of the two naturally round lakes in the world.

Dr. John Gorrie of Apalachicola invented mechanical refrigeration and air conditioning in 1851.

Some cities and counties are in the Eastern Time Zone but those south of Alabama are in the Central Time Zone.

The famous Blue Angels flight demonstration team make their home in Pensacola.

The National Museum of Naval Aviation is located in Pensacola.

Some Tarzan movies featuring Johnny Weissmuller and Maureen O'Sullivan were filmed at Wakulla Springs.

State University System

The state university system is comprised of 12 institutions. Below is a list of the different universities that make up the state system:

- Florida Agricultural and Mechanical University (Tallahassee)
- Florida Atlantic University (Boca Raton)
- Florida Gulf Coast University (Fort Myers)
- Florida International University (Miami)
- Florida Polytechnic University (Lakeland)
- Florida State University (Tallahassee)
- New College of Florida (Sarasota)
- University of Central Florida (Orlando)
- University of Florida (Gainesville)
- University of North Florida (Jacksonville)
- University of South Florida (Tampa)
- University of West Florida (Pensacola)

Florida College System

Florida's colleges remain the primary point of access to higher education in Florida, with 65 percent of the state's high school graduates pursuing postsecondary education beginning at a Florida college and 82 percent of freshman and sophomore minority students in public higher education attending one of Florida's 28 colleges. The 28 colleges are:

- Broward College (Davie)
- Chipola College (Marianna)
- College of Central Florida (Ocala)
- Daytona State College (Daytona Beach)
- Eastern Florida State College (Cocoa)
- Florida Gateway College (Lake City)
- Florida Keys Community College (Key West)
- Florida State College at Jacksonville (Jacksonville)
- Florida SouthWestern State College (Fort Myers)

- Gulf Coast State College (Panama City)
- Hillsborough Community College (Tampa)
- Indian River State College (Ft. Pierce)
- Lake-Sumter State College (Leesburg)
- Miami Dade College (Miami)
- North Florida Community College (Madison)
- Northwest Florida State College (Niceville)
- Palm Beach State College (Lake Worth)
- Pasco-Hernando State College (New Port Richey)
- Pensacola State College (Pensacola)
- Polk State College (Winter Haven)
- Santa Fe College (Gainesville)
- Seminole State College of Florida (Sanford)
- South Florida State College (Avon Park)
- St. Johns River State College (Palatka)
- St. Petersburg College (St. Petersburg)
- State College of Florida, Manatee-Sarasota (Bradenton)
- Tallahassee Community College (Tallahassee)
- Valencia College (Orlando)

Independent Colleges and Universities

The Independent Colleges and Universities of Florida (ICUF) is an association of 30 private education institutions in the state of Florida. A list of these follows:

- Adventist University of Health Sciences (Orlando)
- Ave Maria University (Ave Maria/Naples)
- Barry University (Miami Shores)
- Beacon College (Leesburg)
- Bethune-Cookman University (Daytona Beach)
- Eckerd College (St. Petersburg)
- Edward Waters College (Jacksonville)
- Embry-Riddle Aeronautical University (Daytona Beach)
- Everglades University (Boca Raton)
- Flagler College (St. Augustine)
- Florida College (Temple Terrace)
- Florida Institute of Technology (Melbourne)

IN-STATE TUITION POLICY

To be classified as a "resident for tuition purposes," a person or, if a dependent child, the child's parent or parents shall have established legal residence in Florida and **shall have maintained legal residence in Florida for at least twelve (12) consecutive months immediately prior to his or her initial enrollment**...Every applicant for admission to a university shall be required to make a statement as to the length of residence in the state and, shall also establish his or her presence, or, if a dependent child, the presence of his or her parent or parents, in the state for the purpose of maintaining a bona fide domicile in accordance with the provisions of the statute.

....

An individual shall **not** be classified as a resident for tuition purposes and, thus, shall **not** be eligible to receive the resident tuition rate until the individual has provided satisfactory evidence as to his or her legal residence and domicile to appropriate university officials. In determining residency, the university shall require evidence such as:

- A Florida voter registration card.
- A Florida driver license.
- A State of Florida identification card.
- A Florida vehicle registration.
- Proof of a permanent home in Florida which is occupied as a primary residence by the individual or by the individual's parent if the individual is a dependent child.
- Proof of a homestead exemption in Florida.
- Transcripts from a Florida high school for multiple years if the Florida high school diploma or GED was earned within the last 12 months.
- Proof of permanent full-time employment in Florida for at least 30 hrs/week for a 12-month period.
- A declaration of domicile in Florida.
- A Florida professional or occupational license.
- Florida incorporation.
- A document evidencing family ties in Florida.
- Proof of membership in a Florida-based charitable or professional organization.
- Any other documentation that supports the student's request for resident status including but not limited to: utility bills and proof of 12 consecutive months of payments; a lease agreement and proof of 12 consecutive months of payments; or an official state, federal or court document evidencing legal ties to Florida.

Source: Florida Statute § 240.1201, Determination of resident status for tuition purposes. Read the entire statute online at http://www.leg.state.fl.us/

- Florida Memorial University (Miami)
- Florida Southern College (Lakeland)
- Hodges University (Naples)
- Jacksonville University (Jacksonville)
- Keiser University (Miami)
- Lynn University (Boca Raton)
- Nova Southeastern University (Davie)
- Palm Beach Atlantic University (West Palm Beach)
- Ringling College of Art and Design (Sarasota)
- Rollins College (Winter Park)
- Saint Leo University (St. Leo)
- Saint Thomas University (Miami Gardens)
- Southeastern University (Lakeland)
- Stetson University (Deland)
- University of Miami (Coral Gables)
- University of Tampa (Tampa)
- Warner University (Lake Wales)
- Webber International University (Babson Park)

Additionally, 20 colleges and universities are not affiliated with the ICUF but are fully accredited universities in the state of Florida. They are:

- Baptist College of Florida (Graceville)
- Carlos Albizu University (Miami)
- Digital Media Arts College (Boca Raton)
- Everest University (Pompano Beach)
- Florida Christian College (Kissimmee)
- Florida National College (Hialeah)
- Fort Lauderdale Institute of Art (Fort Lauderdale)
- Full Sail University (Winter Park)
- Hobe Sound Bible College (Hobe Sound)
- Johnson & Wales University (North Miami)
- Jones College (Jacksonville)
- Miami International University of Art & Design (Sarasota)
- Northwood University (West Palm Beach)
- Orlando Culinary Academy (Orlando)
- Pensacola Christian College (Pensacola)

- Rasmussen College (Holiday, Ocala, Fort Myers)
- Saint John Vianney College Seminary (Miami)
- Schiller International University (Largo)
- Trinity College (Temple Terrace)
- University of South Florida Sarasota (Sarasota)

Scholarships and Financial Aid

Florida residents have access to many different scholarships and grants to further education. One of the most popular among graduating high school seniors is the Florida Bright Futures Scholarship. In 1997, the Florida Legislature created the Florida Bright Futures Scholarship Program to reward students for their academic achievements during high school by providing funding to attend postsecondary education facilities in Florida.

The Florida Bright Futures Scholarship Program is comprised of the following four awards:

- Florida Academic Scholars award at $103 per credit hour
- Florida Medallion Scholars award at $77 per credit hour
- Florida Gold Seal Vocational Scholars award at $77 per credit hour
- The Academic Top Scholars award at $44 per credit hour

You can find more information on the Bright Futures Scholarship and additional scholarship programs at www.floridastudentfinancialaid.org.

Out-of-State Tuition Waived for Veterans

To boost residency and the quality of its workforce, Florida passed Senate Bill 0084, which went into effect on July 1, 2014, and provides veterans with in-state tuition rates for education obtained at a state university or Florida College System institution. This effectively waives out-of-state tuition fees and its residency requirements for veterans making a new home in Florida and registering for classes. The bill applies to certain veterans of the Armed Forces of the United States, including the National Guard and reserve components.

Top 5 Florida Institutions of Higher Education by Enrollment

Miami Dade College is a public four-year college with eight campuses and 21 outreach centers located throughout Miami-Dade County. It is the largest member institution of the Florida College System. Miami Dade College's main campus is in downtown Miami. Founded in 1959 as Dade County Junior College, it is the largest nonprofit institution of higher education in Florida and the second-largest in the United States with over 165,000 students. Miami Dade College offers degrees for associates and bachelors, programs in vocational trades as well as certifications.

The programs the college offers include accounting, agriculture, atmospheric science and meteorology, building construction, dietetics, business administration, economics, engineering, forestry, pre-law and pre-veterinary medicine.

University of Central Florida is a metropolitan public research university located in Orlando. UCF is a member institution of the State University System of Florida and is currently the largest university in the state and the third largest university in the United States by enrollment.

UCF is a space-grant university and has made noted research contributions to optics, modeling and simulation, digital media, engineering and computer science, business administration, education and hospitality management. University of Central Florida offers bachelors, masters and doctoral degrees in various fields.

The programs offered include diversity, business, accounting, social sciences and education. Founded in 1963 as Florida Technological University, this school's original goal was to provide highly trained personnel to support the Kennedy Space Center. As the university's academic scope expanded to encompass other disciplines, the school was renamed the University of Central Florida in 1978.

University of Florida is an American public land-grant, sea-grant, space-grant research university located on a 2,000-acre campus in Gainesville. The university traces its origins to 1853 and has operated continuously on its present Gainesville campus since September 1906. UF is currently ranked 50th overall in national universities, public and private, and ranks among the world's top 100 universities. It is the third largest Florida university by student population and the most academically prestigious university in the state of Florida, as measured by national and international rankings of American colleges and universities. It is also one of the most academically diverse in the nation, as measured by the number of academic programs offered and is home to 16 academic colleges and more than 150 research centers and institutes. The school offers multiple graduate professional programs including business administration, engineering, law and medicine on one contiguous campus and administers 150 master's degree programs and 76 doctoral degree programs in 87 schools and departments.

University of South Florida is a member institution of the State University System of Florida and is one of the state's three flagship universities. It is a public research university located in Tampa with an autonomous campus in St. Petersburg and branch centers in Sarasota and Lakeland. Founded in 1956, USF is the fourth largest university in the state of Florida. The programs offered at University of South Florida include business, education, criminal justice, engineering, music, nursing, law, medicine, social work, human services and communication. USF has 18 colleges, schools and institutions.

Florida State University is a space-grant and sea-grant public university located in Tallahassee. FSU is a comprehensive doctoral research university with medical programs. The university comprises 16 separate colleges and 39 centers, facilities, labs and institutes that offer more than 300 programs of study. Florida State is a flagship university in the State University System of Florida. As one of Florida's primary graduate research universities, Florida State awards over 2,000 graduate and professional degrees each year.

FSU is home to nationally ranked programs in many academic areas, including the sciences, social policy, film, engineering, the arts, business, political science, social work, medicine and law. Florida State is home to Florida's only National Laboratory, the National High Magnetic Field Laboratory, and is the birthplace of the commercially viable, anti-cancer drug Taxol. FSU was officially established in 1851 and is located on the oldest continuous site of higher education in the state of Florida.

Florida Careers

The Sunshine State can boast of its warm weather and beautiful beaches and also of a job growth rate that is more than double the national average and a very low unemployment rate. Nearly every major industry is experiencing growth in Florida. The areas with the largest number of new jobs in Florida are Miami/Fort Lauderdale, Orlando and Tampa/St. Petersburg.

Technology careers are hot in Florida. The top seven jobs expected to experience significant growth in the next decade are computer software specialists, computer software applications engineers, network administrators, computer systems software engineers, desktop publishers, systems analysts and database administrators.

Health and medical professionals are in high demand in Florida. According to the Orlando Sentinel (www.orlandosentinel.com), the positions in greatest demand are physician assistants, medical assistants, medical records and health information technicians, physical therapy aides, respiratory therapy technicians, occupational therapy assistants, home health aides, registered nurses, pharmacy technicians, mental health and substance abuse social workers.

"HEY, PETE - I FOUND A SET OF TRACKS."

"I have a very strict gun control policy: if there's a gun around, I want to be in control of it."
–Clint Eastwood

CHAPTER 13

OWNING A FIREARM IN FLORIDA

Packing and transporting an entire life's worth of possessions to Florida is no small task, especially if it involves large collections of valuable items like artwork, cars or firearms. Each item in your home requires a different level of attention and care. While all possessions are property, transporting firearms to Florida may present the most unique challenge. To this end, we have put together some information about gun ownership in Florida to ease the transition.

Protecting Your Collection

Typically, collections of significant value are not covered under homeowners insurance. Homeowners insurance will generally list personal property as "coverage C." While coverage C insures all the belongings inside a home, it is usually set at a limited amount. And, in many cases, there may also be sub-limits within the policy. Because of this, homeowners should consult with an insurance agent to determine the terms of coverage.

In most cases involving large firearm collections, you will need to add coverage to your existing policy (a rider) or obtain additional insurance from an insurer that specializes in valuable collectables.

The best way to know how much coverage you should have can be determined with an appraisal to ensure that the limits of your policy meet the current market value of your collection. After an appraisal is completed, it is a good idea to create a catalog of your collection. A catalog allows you to make more accurate insurance claims and can also help itemize and track serial numbers or provide details as to where each item is stored.

For gun owners, insuring your gun collection is a good first step. However, as a new Florida resident, you may want to consider also insuring yourself. For example, in the event of a self-defense shooting, the person who used force in self-defense may be required to defend themselves in court in cases where the justifiable use of force is in dispute. On June 9, 2017, Governor Rick Scott signed a bill into law that shifts the burden of proof from the defendants to the prosecution, thus making the use of force justified until proven otherwise. However, this could be a lengthy and expensive process. Self-defense insurance is often purchased by gun owners who have a concealed weapon license. Cost and coverage options vary so it is recommended you obtain numerous quotes before selecting a self-defense insurance policy.

Florida Gun Owner Rights

If you are planning to add to your firearms collection as a Florida resident, it is important to be aware of those laws that govern and relate to the possession and/or purchase of firearms in Florida. While the State of Florida does not require a permit to possess or purchase a rifle, shotgun or handgun, it does have several specific restrictions when it comes to purchasing a firearm. To understand how Florida gun laws evolved, let's look at Federal firearms history.

The original National Firearms Act of 1934 imposed a tax on the making and transfer of specific firearms. The law also required that all the firearms and weapons defined by the Act be registered with the Secretary of Treasury. Congress found that the firearms defined by this Act posed a significant crime problem because they were frequently used in gangland crimes of the era. Firearms that the 1934 Act included were shotguns and rifles with barrels less than 18 inches, machine guns, firearm mufflers, silencers and certain firearms described as "any other weapons." To curb the crime problems, Congress imposed a $200 tax on the making and transfer of these weapons.

Legislation surrounding the National Firearms Act of 1934 was amended in 1968 and now requires people who wish to purchase the types of weapons listed in the original act to follow a special process. There are many weapons that fall under the umbrella of "National Firearms Act" that may require additional fees and registration with the Bureau of Alcohol, Tobacco and Firearms (also known as BATF or simply ATF) under the National Firearms Act, Title II of the Gun Control Act of 1968. A full list of these weapons can be found on the ATF website, www.atf.gov. It is recommended that you make yourself aware of the firearms, weapons and accessories in this category to make a proper assessment of the time and financial commitment it may take to purchase these items.

Age is a factor that may restrict a person's ability to purchase a gun. A person 18 years of age or older has the ability to purchase a rifle or shotgun, generally referred to as a "long gun." Florida law does not require a special permit or fingerprints to purchase a long gun but does conduct a background check utilizing demographic data provided by the BATF Form 4473. Florida law does not require a waiting period for the purchase of a long gun; however, individual counties, cities and municipalities do have the ability to add to or lengthen the waiting period.

To purchase a handgun in the State of Florida, you must be at least 21 years old. A handgun is defined as any firearm that is capable of being carried and used by one hand. Fingerprints and special permits are not required but there will be at least a three-day waiting period for those without a concealed weapon license. Please check your local regulations for specific details regarding your area's waiting period.

Florida does not allow "open carry" unless you are covered by one of a few exceptions generally limited to law enforcement officers or if you are traveling to or from a location where the gun has a reasonable purpose (i.e., a gun range). Section 790.053 of the Florida Statutes includes more examples of such specific situations.

In Florida, gun owners may apply for a concealed weapon license if all the proper steps are taken (see pages 230-233).

SIX-STEPS TO GUN OWNERSHIP

1. Select a firearm from a licensed gun dealer.
2. Fill out the Bureau of Alcohol, Tobacco and Firearms (BATF) Form 4473. This form will be provided by the gun dealer and will be used to conduct a background check. Visit www.atf.gov for more information.
3. The dealer will require you to present a valid form of government issued identification as well as any non-resident forms of identification.
4. The dealer will then contact the Firearm Purchase Program at the Florida Department of Law Enforcement.
5. An operator from the Firearm Purchase Program will validate data on your BATF Form 4473 and determine your eligibility.
6. The dealer is provided with a transaction identification number and a decision on the transaction.

Source: Bureau of Alcohol, Tobacco and Firearms

Growing Your Collection in Florida

Approximately one Florida resident in three owns a gun in Florida. Thus, the state of Florida provides a friendly atmosphere for serious gun collectors. The process of obtaining new firearms in Florida is relatively straightforward (see Six-Steps on page 228). To simplify the process, seek an experienced gun collector for advice.

Be aware that Florida law requires firearm dealers to comply with a mandatory three-day waiting period for handgun sales unless the purchaser is a concealed weapon license holder.

No Gun for You

Firearm sales can be denied to any person for one or more of the following reasons according to the Florida Department of Law Enforcement:

- Felony conviction
- Active warrant, felony or misdemeanor
- Unlawful user or addicted to any controlled substance
- Adjudicated mentally defective or involuntarily committed by a judge
- Illegal alien status
- Dishonorable discharge from U.S. Armed Forces
- Renounced United States citizenship
- Active protection order (injunction for protection, restraining order, etc.)
- Convicted of a misdemeanor crime of domestic violence
- Under indictment for a crime punishable by a term exceeding one year in prison

- Adjudicated delinquent or received adjudication withheld as a juvenile for a felony charge and is a person under the age of 24
- Adjudication withheld for any felony or a misdemeanor crime of domestic violence and three years has not yet lapsed since the completion of sentencing provisions

Do I Need a Concealed Weapon License?

In the State of Florida, concealed weapon licenses are becoming more and more common. According to Jeb Bush in a speech to the National Rifle Association in 2015, Florida has the most concealed weapon permits in the nation, "nearly double that of the second state, which is Texas." In fact, as of May 31, 2017, there were 1,755,746 active concealed weapon or firearms licenses in Florida. To be granted a concealed weapon license, you must first determine your eligibility. A full list of the disqualifying factors is in the section below. In general, you must be at least 21 years old, demonstrate competency with a firearm and must currently reside in the United States and be a U.S. citizen or be deemed a lawful permanent resident alien.

LICENSE OR PERMIT?

The terms "concealed weapon license" and "concealed weapon permit" are used interchangeably depending on which document you are reading. These are generally synonymous terms that represent the same item. Here are some other terms used by the media and public when referring to this issue:

- Conceal carry
- Concealed weapons permit
- Campus carry

Concealed Carry Disqualifiers

The following list outlines the disqualifying factors as set by the Florida Department of Agriculture, the arm of the State government that issues concealed weapon licenses.

- The physical inability to handle a firearm safely
- A felony conviction (unless civil and firearm rights have been restored by the convicting authority)
- Having adjudication withheld or sentence suspended on a felony or misdemeanor crime of violence unless three years have elapsed since probation or other conditions set by the court have been fulfilled
- A conviction for a misdemeanor crime of violence in the last three years
- A conviction for violation of controlled substance laws or multiple arrests for such offenses
- A record of drug or alcohol abuse
- Two or more DUI convictions within the previous three years
- Being committed to a mental institution or adjudged incompetent or mentally defective
- Failing to provide proof of proficiency with a firearm
- Having been issued a domestic violence injunction or an injunction against repeat violence that is currently in force
- Renouncement of U.S. citizenship
- A dishonorable discharge from the armed forces
- Being a fugitive from justice

Obtaining a Concealed Weapon Permit

There are many courses offered in Florida that you can take to fulfill the competency requirement portion of the concealed weapon license application. They are:

- Any hunter education or hunter safety course approved by Florida Fish and Wildlife Conservation Commission or similar agency in another state,
- Any NRA firearms safety or training course or
- A firearms training or safety course or class conducted by a state-certified instructor.

A full list of acceptable courses you can complete to demonstrate competency can be found at www.freshfromflorida.com.

After determining your eligibility, you will need to determine how you want to apply. You may apply at a Department of Agriculture and Consumer Services regional office, at an authorized Florida tax collector's office or by mail.

If you intend to apply in person, you will need to call ahead and make an appointment. There is no need to complete an application prior to your appointment. You will complete an application during your appointment. Be sure to bring a photo ID, a copy of a training document or other certification that confirms you are proficient with a firearm and your payment. Keep in mind that some government agency offices cannot accept cash. You will also be fingerprinted which is an additional cost.

Applying by mail may take longer but the process is fairly simple. Download the Concealed Weapon or Firearm Licenses Application instructions on www.freshfromflorida.com.

Once you know the steps, you can download and complete a Concealed Weapon or Firearm Licenses Application. You will need to schedule an appointment with your local sheriff's office to be fingerprinted (there will be a fee associated with this). Be sure to get the facilitating officer's signature on the fingerprint card.

Mail your original application, the signed fingerprint card and a copy of a photo ID (driver license or state-issued ID is acceptable) to:

Florida Department of Agriculture and Consumer Services
Division of Licensing
P.O. Box 6687
Tallahassee, FL 32314-6687

What is Carry Reciprocity?

Florida has reciprocity agreements with most states allowing you to continue to carry a concealed weapon as you normally would in those states—as long as you comply with Florida law. However, if you are taking steps to change your domicile to Florida and you have either 1.) registered to vote, 2.) made a declaration of domicile or 3.) filed for homestead tax exemption on property in Florida, your concealed weapon license will remain active for 90 days following the date of the first task you completed of the three items listed above. Consult the chart below to confirm that your former state's concealed carry laws are recognized by the state of Florida.

Understanding "Stand Your Ground"

Self-defense laws vary in specific wording throughout the nation but generally fall into one of two categories: 1.) stand your ground and 2.) duty to retreat. In its most pure form, duty to retreat means that a person must retreat from an imminent threat as much as possible before responding with force in self-defense. Stand your ground essentially removes the duty to retreat wording from the justifiable use-of-force laws.

According to the 2016 Florida Statutes, a person is justified in using force, excluding deadly force, when that person reasonably believes it is necessary to protect themselves from another's imminent use of force. The use of deadly force is justified only when it is believed necessary to prevent imminent death or great bodily injury to themselves or another. In either situation, under

Florida law, you do not have a duty to retreat from an attacker when you are in any place that you are lawfully allowed to be present. For example, if you are at a park and are attacked, you have the right to stand your ground and defend yourself with the appropriate force if you believe that it is necessary to prevent bodily harm to another person or yourself.

Florida is also one of 22 states that provide civil immunity in certain self-defense circumstances.

Castle Doctrine

Something commonly associated with stand your ground law is the "Castle Doctrine." In general, this term defines a person's home as their castle and gives them the right to defend it without a duty to retreat. Florida's version of this common law is covered in Section 776.013 of the Florida Statutes. Regarding home protection, this Statute states that:

> *A person is presumed to have held a reasonable fear of imminent peril of death or great bodily harm to himself or herself or another when using or threatening to use defensive force that is intended or likely to cause death or great bodily harm to another if:*
>
> *(a) The person against whom the defensive force was used or threatened was in the process of unlawfully and forcefully entering, or had unlawfully and forcibly entered, a dwelling, residence, or occupied vehicle, or if that person had removed or was attempting to remove another person against that person's will from the dwelling, residence, or occupied vehicle; and*
>
> *(b) The person who uses or threatens to use defensive force knew or had reason to believe that an unlawful and forcible entry or unlawful and forcible act was occurring or had occurred.*

Table: Florida Gun Laws Recognized by Other States

STATE	Stand Your Ground	Concealed Carry Reciprocity
Alabama	Yes	Yes
Alaska	Yes	Yes
Arizona	Yes	Yes
Arkansas	No	Yes
California	No	No
Colorado	No	Yes
Conecticut	No	No
Delaware	No	Yes
Georgia	Yes	Yes
Hawaii	No	No
Idaho	No	Yes
Illinois	No	No
Indiana	Yes	Yes
Iowa	No	Yes
Kansas	Yes	Yes
Kentucky	Yes	Yes
Louisiana	Yes	Yes
Maine	No	Yes
Maryland	No	No
Massachusetts	No	No
Michigan	Yes	Yes
Minnesota	No	No
Mississippi	Yes	Yes
Missouri	No	Yes
Montana	Yes	Yes
Nebraska	No	Yes
Nevada	Yes	Yes
New Hampshire	Yes	Yes
New Jersey	No	No
New Mexico	No	Yes
New York	No	No
North Carolina	Yes	Yes
North Dakota	No	Yes
Ohio	Yes	Yes
Oklahoma	No	Yes
Oregon	No	No
Pennsylvania	Yes	Yes
Rhode Island	No	No
South Carolina	Yes	Yes
South Dakota	Yes	Yes
Tennessee	Yes	Yes
Texas	Yes	Yes
Utah	Yes	Yes
Vermont	No	Yes
Virginia	Yes	Yes
Washington	No	No
West Virginia	Yes	Yes
Wisconsin	No	No
Wyoming	No	Yes

Source: Florida Department of Agriculture and Consumer Services

There are several stipulations that would disqualify use of castle doctrine including 1.) if the person against whom the defensive force is threatened has a lawful right to be there, 2.) if that person is a child or grandchild of the person seeking the removal, 3.) if the person who threatens the use of force is engaged in criminal activity or 4.) if the person against whom force is used or threatened is a law enforcement officer.

Recreational Gun Use

After you have become familiar with Florida's firearms laws, you will find Florida is a great state in which to be a firearms enthusiast. As a popular retirement destination, Florida is filled with a growing army of collectors and experts who have decades of specialty knowledge and ownership experience.

Gun collecting is a very popular hobby. Like most other collectibles industries, there are as many sub-genres as there are enthusiasts. Finding new friends with similar gun collecting interests can help make your transition to Florida a pleasant experience. Local gun shop and shooting range owners and/or employees are great resources for those looking for niche clubs.

Another obvious place to find firearms enthusiasts is at gun shows. Many members take advantage of these shows to organize meetings or set up booths to recruit new members. Fortunately, there is an abundance of gun shows across the state where enthusiasts can buy, trade, sell or just browse different makes and models with like-minded people.

Gun Show Etiquette

Most major gun show promoters in Florida take safety very seriously and require all weapons, including those being carried by individuals with a concealed weapon license, be checked by a law enforcement officer prior to entering. The weapon is fitted with a plastic tie to prevent it from firing during your visit. Other promoters have been known to require all show guests adhere to its unloaded, two-gun maximum.

Where to Discharge a Firearm

Florida is home to many gun ranges, both indoor and outdoor, that provide a variety of experiences. For example, travel to Orlando and you can shoot to thrill at Machine Gun America. There are target and skeet ranges in just about every county, too. Some ranges host special services and events including Ladies Night, ballistics seminars, gunsmithing classes and concealed carry courses.

There are also nine Florida Fish & Wildlife managed ranges, with an additional two currently being constructed in Florida. In addition to rifle, shotgun, pistol and archery ranges, many of these facilities also provide sporting clay classes and tournaments.

Hunting with Firearms

If you are a fan of using a firearm when you hunt animals, then you will be pleased to discover that Florida has a robust hunting season. Florida is segmented into four hunting zones: A, B, C and D. Hunting seasons vary in each zone so be sure to check the Florida Fish and Wildlife Conservation Commission chart as a guide. The zone chart and season matrix can be found at www.myfwc.com.

Before you venture outdoors to hunt and shoot your dinner, you must possess a valid hunting license. The Florida Fish and Wildlife Conservation Commission provides a Florida Resident Sportsman's License which costs around $80. Hunting licenses are good for one year and satisfy all state requirements for recreational hunting and freshwater fishing for Florida residents. Included in this license is: resident hunting, resident freshwater fishing, archers, muzzle loading, state waterfowl, turkey and access to any of the nearly 6 million acres of wildlife management areas via a management stamp. For a full list of wildlife management areas, visit www.myfwc.com.

Interestingly, you do not need a hunting license if you are a resident who is 65 years of age or older or are a resident who is 100% disabled (must present a letter from your doctor to obtain an exemption card from the Tax Collector's office). Be sure to have your proof of age and residency handy if approached by any Game and Fish agent.

Keep in mind that not all land is available for hunting and different public lands have different regulations that hunters must follow.

Florida hosts hunting seasons for the following animals: deer, Spring and Fall turkey, gray squirrel, quail, rabbit, wild hog, bobcat, otter, raccoon, opossum, coyote, beaver, skunk and nutria. Season open and close dates may vary slightly from year to year, so you should consult www.myfwc.com for the latest list. Please note that some of these animals require a special tag to hunt and have strict limits.

Before packing up and heading out to your favorite woodland destination for a hunting trip, it is recommended that you check all of your hunting equipment and ensure it is in proper working order. It may also be wise to familiarize yourself with any new equipment you plan to bring.

Because completing a hunting safety course is a prerequisite to obtaining a hunting license, you should be familiar with general safety practices. If you wish to refresh your memory, hunting safety tips and regulations are available at www.myfwc.com. After double checking equipment and ensuring that you are up-to-date on all safety guidelines, all that is left to do is to choose an acceptable location and an in-season animal to hunt.

FLORIDA HUNTING SEASONS

Deer:
Zone A: Sept. 16 - Oct. 15 and Nov. 18 - Jan. 7
Zone B: Dec. 2 - Feb. 18
Zone C: Nov. 4 - Jan. 21
Zone D: Nov. 23 - 26 and Dec. 9 - Feb. 18

Fall Turkey:
Zone A: Oct. 9 - 15 and Nov. 18 - Jan. 7
Zone B: Dec. 2 - Jan. 28
Zone C: Nov. 4 - Dec. 31
Zone D: Nov. 23 - 26 and Dec. 9 - Jan. 14

Gray Squirrel:
Zone A: Oct. 14 - Mar. 4
Zone B: Oct. 14 - Mar. 4
Zone C: Oct. 14 - Mar. 4
Zone D: Oct. 14 - Mar. 4

Quail:
Zone A: Nov. 11 - Mar. 4
Zone B: Nov. 11 - Mar. 4
Zone C: Nov. 11 - Mar. 4
Zone D: Nov. 11 - Mar. 4

Spring Turkey:
South of State Road 70: Mar. 3 - Apr. 8
North of State Road 70: Mar. 17 - Apr. 22

Statewide, year-round:
Rabbit, Wild Hog, Bobcat, Otter, Raccoon, Coyote, Beaver, Skunk, Nutria

APPENDIX A
ONLINE RESOURCES

STATE INFORMATION

The Official Website for the State of Florida: www.myflorida.com

Current Facts on Florida: www.flheritage.com/facts

Florida Official Vacation Guide Web Site: www.visitflorida.com

Florida Chamber of Commerce: www.floridachamber.com

Florida Realtors: www.floridarealtors.org

Florida Weather and Hurricane Center: www.nhc.noaa.gov

Florida Division of Emergency Management: www.floridadisaster.org

Change of Mailing Address: https://moversguide.usps.com

Division of Elections: http://election.dos.state.fl.us/

State Parks: http://www.floridastateparks.org/

Florida Statutes: http://www.leg.state.fl.us/

LOCAL INFORMATION

Florida Churches: www.churchangel.com/florida.htm

Florida Cities: www.floridaleagueofcities.com

Florida Counties: www.myfloridacounty.com

Clerk of Courts Listing: www.myfloridacounty.com

APPENDIX A: ONLINE RESOURCES

BOATING

Florida Boating Safety: www.FloridaBoatingCourse.com
Safety Equipment Requirements for Florida Watercraft:
www.myfwc.com

BUSINESS

Doing Business in Florida: www.eflorida.com
Florida Business Guide: www.floridabusinessguide.com
Employment and Labor Issues: www.floridajobs.org
Career Opportunities:
www.indeed.com/l-Florida-jobs.html
www.jobs.careerbuilder.com
www.floridacareers.com
www.floridajobs.org
www.employflorida.com
https://jobs.myflorida.com

EDUCATION

Florida Department of Education: www.fldoe.org
Florida Residency for Tuition Purposes:
www.flbog.edu/forstudents/ati/resrequirements.php
Florida Department of Education, Student Financial Assistance:
www.floridastudentfinancialaid.org
Florida Scholarships: www.floridastudentfinancialaid.org
Public School Rankings: www.greatschools.org/florida/
Voluntary Prekindergarten: www.vpkhelp.org

EMERGENCY MANAGEMENT

Shelters/Evacuation Routes:
http://www.floridadisaster.org/DEMpublic.asp
Post-Disaster Assistance: www.disasterassistance.gov
Report a Wildfire: (850) 413-9900

FIREARMS

Determine which states accept your Florida Concealed Carry Permit:
https://www.concealedcarry.com/dynamic-ccw-permit-reciprocity-map-builder/

Map of shooting ranges in Florida:
https://www.shooting.org/Ranges/Florida
https://rangelistings.com/shooting-ranges/FL.html

List of FWC managed public shooting ranges:
http://myfwc.com/hunting/safety-education/shooting-ranges/

FISHING/HUNTING

Fishing License Information: http://myfwc.com/fishing
Fish & Wildlife Conservation Commission: www.myfwc.com
Freshwater Fishing: http://myfwc.com/license/
Saltwater Fishing: http://myfwc.com/license/
Hunting in Florida: http://myfwc.com/hunting/

HEALTH

Health Insurance, Office of Insurance Regulation:
www.floir.com
Insurance Companies: www.floir.com/companysearch/
Health Care Facilities: www.FloridaHealthFinder.gov
Health Care Information: www.fdhc.state.fl.us
Hospitals and Health Systems:
www.fha.org/reports-and-resources/hospital-directory.aspx
Health Care Assistance for Children:
Florida Kid Care: www.floridakidcare.org
Healthy Kids: www.healthykids.org
Senior Pharmacy Resources/Prescription Drug Assistance:
www.floridahealthfinder.gov/index.html

MOTOR VEHICLES

Driver License Offices: www.flhsmv.gov/locations/
First Time Drivers: www.firsttimedriver.com

APPENDIX A: ONLINE RESOURCES

Department of Highway Safety &Motor Vehicles:
www.hsmv.state.fl.us
SunPass: www.sunpass.com
Vehicle Tags and Registration: www.hsmv.state.fl.us/html/titlinf.html
Traffic School: www.floridadrivingcourse.com

REAL ESTATE

www.realtor.com
http://fl.living.net
www.trulia.com
www.zillow.com

TAXES, FINANCES, PROPERTY INSURANCE

Florida Department of Revenue: www.myflorida.com/dor
Florida Taxes/Florida Tax Guide:
www.myflorida.com/dor/gta.html
Department of Revenue, Business Division:
http://dor.myflorida.com/dor/businesses/
Florida Tax-Related Information: www.myflorida.com/dor
Department of Financial Services, Consumer Guides:
www.myfloridacfo.com/Division/Consumers/
Florida Statutes: www.flsenate.gov/statutes
Citizens Property Insurance Corporation: www.citizensfla.com
Charity Verification Service: http://www.guidestar.org

U.S. GOVERNMENT

Social Security/Medicare: https://www.ssa.gov/
U.S. Citizenship & Immigration Issues: www.uscis.gov
U.S. Government Forms (FEMA, VA benefits, etc.):
www.forms.gov
Passport (new or renewal): www.travel.state.gov
Federal Voting Assistance Program: www.fvap.gov

VOTER REGISTRATION

Florida Voter Registration Information:
http://election.dos.state.fl.us/voter-registration/voter-reg.shtml

APPENDIX B1
DECLARATION OF FLORIDA DOMICILE - *SAMPLE*

DECLARATION OF DOMICILE

To the Clerk of the Circuit Court of ____________
This is my DECLARATION OF DOMICILE in the STATE OF FLORIDA that I am filing this day in Accordance and in conformity with Florida Statute Section 222.17.
I hereby declare that I reside in and maintain a place of abode at

____
Street and Number

____________________, FL ________
City and County Zip Code

Which place of abode I recognize and intend to maintain as my permanent home and, if I maintain another place or places of abode in some other state or states. I hereby declare that my above described residence and abode in the State of Florida constitutes my predominant and principal home, and I intend to continue it permanently as such. I am at the time of making this declaration, a bona fide resident of the State of Florida.

I formerly resided at:

____
Street and Number

____
City, County, State, and Zip Code

And the place or places where I maintain another or other place or places of abode are as follows: (in the space provided, list address, city, county, and state of any other place(s)

____
Signature

____
Print Name

State of Florida
County of ____________

Sworn to and subscribed before me this __________ day of ____________________, _________, by the above named, who ____ is personally known to me or _____ has produced the following type of identification:

Clerk of the Circuit Court

______________________________ ______________________________
Signature of Notary Signature of Deputy Clerk

______________________________ ______________________________
Printed Name of Notary Printed Name of Deputy Clerk

APPENDIX B2
FLORIDA HOMESTEAD (*AD VALOREM*) TAX EXEMPTION (FORM DR 501) - *SAMPLE*

For visual representation ONLY. **NOTE:** There are 3 pages to this form.

FLORIDA DEPARTMENT OF REVENUE

ORIGINAL APPLICATION FOR HOMESTEAD AND RELATED TAX EXEMPTIONS

DR-501
R. 12/12
Rule 12D-16.002, F.A.C.
Eff. 12/12
Provisional

Permanent Florida residency required on January 1.
Application due to property appraiser by March 1.

County	Tax Year	Parcel ID
I am applying for homestead exemption, $25,000 to $50,000	☐ New ☐ Change	☐ Addition
Do you claim residency in another county or state? Applicant? ☐ Yes ☐ No	Co-applicant? ☐ Yes ☐ No	

	Applicant	Co-applicant/Spouse
Name		
*Social Security #		
Immigration #		
Date of birth		
% of ownership		
Date of occupancy		
Marital status	☐ Single ☐ Married ☐ Divorced ☐ Widowed	

Homestead address	Mailing address, if different
Legal description	Phone
Type of deed ______________ Date of deed _____	Recorded: Book _____ Page _____ Date _____
Did any applicant receive or file for exemptions last year? ☐ Yes ☐ No	
Previous address:	

Please provide as much information as possible. Your county property appraiser will make the final determination.

Proof of Residence	Applicant	Co-applicant/Spouse
Previous residency outside Florida and date terminated	date	date
FL driver license or ID card number	date	date
Evidence of relinquishing driver license from other state		
Florida vehicle tag number		
Florida voter registration number (if US citizen)	date	date
Declaration of domicile, enter date	date	date
Current employer		
Address on your last IRS return		
School location of dependent children		
Bank statement and checking account mailing address		
Proof of payment of utilities at homestead address	☐ Yes ☐ No	☐ Yes ☐ No
Name and address of any owners not residing on the property		

* Disclosure of your social security number is mandatory. It is required by section 196.011(1)(b), Florida Statutes. The social security number will be used to verify taxpayer identity and homestead exemption information submitted to property appraisers.

Continued on page 2

INDEX

Meet Mike Kilbourn

With over 30 years experience in the financial services industry, the last 19 of which have been dedicated to teaching his estate planning strategies to high-net worth families and fellow planners, **E. Michael Kilbourn** knows the intricacies of estate planning and the benefits of Florida domicile.

The president of Kilbourn Associates in Naples, Florida, Mike is a Family Wealth Transfer Planning Specialist who enjoys taking the worry out of wealth and the mystery out of financial planning.

Over the years, Mike has positioned himself as a leading national authority on estate tax matters and as an expert on the complexities of Florida domicile. His sophisticated estate planning abilities have produced remarkable results and secured the trust of hundreds of wealthy individuals and families.

Mike is a decorated Vietnam veteran with five college degrees including four masters' degrees, cum laude, and was inducted into Beta Gamma Sigma. Accredited with fourteen professional designations, including Chartered Financial Consultant and Accredited Estate Planner, he is founder and chairman of the Wealth Protection Network®, a national network of estate-planning professionals.

In addition to co-authoring all editions of *The Florida Domicile Handbook*, Mike is also the co-author of *Disinherit the IRS* (Brendan Kelly Publishing, 2014) and contributing author of *The Four Corners: Where your estate plan becomes a living legacy* (Shared Drive Media, 2012), *Optimal Aging Manual* (Optimal Aging, LLC, 2004), *Giving–Philanthropy for Everyone* (Quantum Press, 2002), *21st Century Wealth: Essential Financial Planning Principles* (Quantum Press, 2000) and *Ways & Means: Maximize the Value of Your Retirement Savings* (Esperti Peterson Institute, 1999).

E. Michael Kilbourn, CLU, ChFC, CCIM, MSFS, CAP, CASL, MBA
Kilbourn Associates
3033 Riviera Drive, Suite 202, Naples, FL 34103
Ph: (239) 261-1888 • Fax: (239) 643-7017
Email: mike@kilbournassociates.com
Website: www.kilbournassociates.com

Meet Brad Galbraith

Brad A. Galbraith, Esq., CPA, is a partner at Woods, Weidenmiller, Michetti, Rudnick & Galbraith, PLLC, and practices at its Naples and Indianapolis offices. Brad is also Chair of the firm's Estate Planning Group. His practice focuses on providing creative, cutting-edge estate, tax and business planning advice to business owners and wealthy individuals. Brad is board certified in Wills, Trusts and Estates by the Florida Bar Association.

Brad began his professional career as a Certified Public Accountant. After switching to the practice of law and seeing the ineffectiveness and inefficiency of traditional planning methods, he endeavored to find a better way to assist his clients with estate, tax and business planning. As an estate-planning attorney, he developed a model designed to provide clients with comprehensive, personalized estate, tax and business succession plans that withstand the test of time.

Brad maintains an Indiana CPA license and is a frequent presenter on estate and tax planning topics to CPAs and attorneys at conferences and continuing education events throughout the United States. Additionally, Brad is the co-author of an extensive continuing education program for CPAs, which was published and distributed nationally. That program, titled Estate Planning for CPAs, has been presented to thousands of CPAs throughout the United States.

Brad is peer review rated as "preeminent" by Martindale Hubbell and is a Florida "Super Lawyer." He is the author or co-author of several books, including *The Florida Domicile Handbook* with Mike Kilbourn, and is active in several national and local charitable and religious organizations.

Brad A. Galbraith, Esq., CPA
Woods, Weidenmiller, Michetti, Rudnick & Galbraith, PLLC
9045 Strada Stell Court, Suite 400, Naples, FL 34109
Ph: (239) 325-4070 • Direct: (239) 325-5581 • Fax: (239) 325-4080
Email: bgalbraith@wwmrglaw.com
Website: www.wwmrglaw.com

Meet Joshua D. Rudnick

Joshua D. Rudnick, Esq., is a partner at Woods, Weidenmiller, Michetti, Rudnick & Galbraith, PLLC, in Naples. His practice is concentrated on commercial and residential real property transactions, construction, corporate and commercial lending.

Josh formerly served as an Assistant State Attorney for the 20th Judicial Circuit. He is currently the President of the Board of Directors for the Mental Health Association of Southwest Florida, a member of the Board of Directors of the Foundation for the Developmentally Disabled and a member of the Advisory Board of the Salvation Army. He also served as chair of the Real Estate Section of the Collier County Bar Association in 2010-2011.

Joshua D. Rudnick, Esq.
Woods, Weidenmiller, Michetti, Rudnick & Galbraith, PLLC
9045 Strada Stell Court, Suite 400, Naples, FL 34109
Ph: (239) 325-4070 • Fax: (239) 325-4080
Email: jrudnick@wwmrglaw.com
Website: www.wwmrglaw.com

Notes

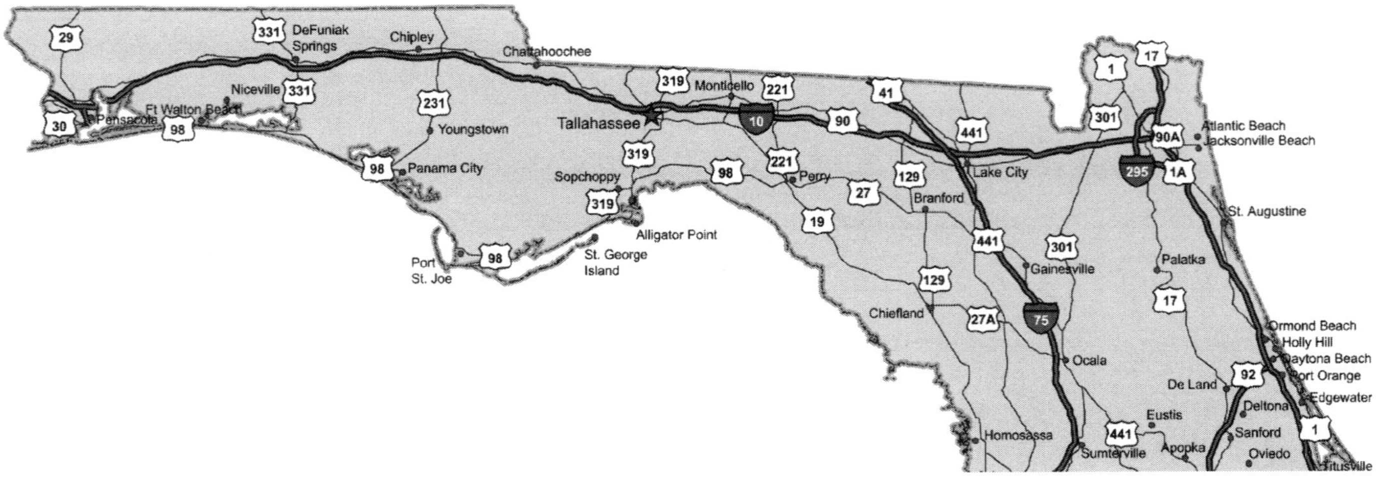
DeFuniak Springs
Chipley
Chattahoochee
Niceville
Ft Walton Beach
Pensacola
Youngstown
Tallahassee
Monticello
Panama City
Sopchoppy
Perry
Branford
Lake City
Alligator Point
St. George Island
Port St. Joe
Chiefland
Gainesville
Ocala
Homosassa
Sumterville
Apopka
Eustis
De Land
Deltona
Sanford
Oviedo
Titusville
Edgewater
Port Orange
Daytona Beach
Holly Hill
Ormond Beach
Palatka
St. Augustine
Atlantic Beach
Jacksonville Beach

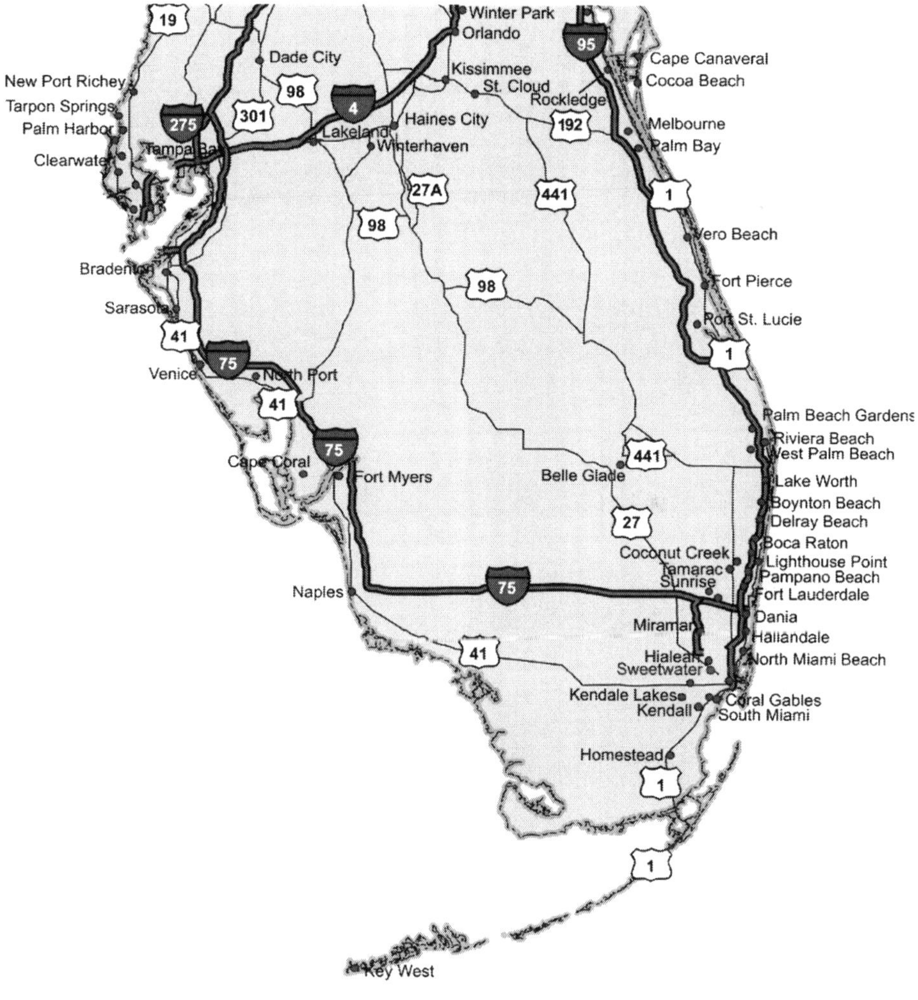

19
Winter Park
Orlando
95
Cape Canaveral
Cocoa Beach
Dade City
Kissimmee
St. Cloud
Rockledge
New Port Richey
98
4
Tarpon Springs
275
301
Haines City
192
Melbourne
Palm Harbor
Lakeland
Palm Bay
Tampa Bay
Winterhaven
Clearwater
27A
441
1
98
Vero Beach
Bradenton
Fort Pierce
98
Sarasota
Port St. Lucie
41
75
1
Venice
North Port
41
Palm Beach Gardens
75
Riviera Beach
West Palm Beach
441
Cape Coral
Fort Myers
Belle Glade
Lake Worth
Boynton Beach
27
Delray Beach
Boca Raton
Coconut Creek
Lighthouse Point
Tamarac
Pampano Beach
Sunrise
Naples
75
Fort Lauderdale
Dania
Miramar
Hallandale
41
Hialeah
North Miami Beach
Sweetwater
Kendale Lakes
Coral Gables
Kendall
South Miami
Homestead
1
1
Key West

Five Steps to Florida!

Take the following five essential steps on your journey to Florida domicile and we promise the rest of the journey will be much easier to navigate. Check off each step as you finish it. See page 116 for complete instructions.

☐ **1.) Declare Domicile.** Fill out and file a declaration of domicile form and either mail or deliver the form to the courthouse in the Florida county in which you reside.

☐ **2.) Obtain a Driver License.** Get a new Florida driver license at a Florida Driver License Bureau office in the county in which you declare domicile.

☐ **3.) Register to Vote.** While getting your driver license, register to vote. This can be done at most Florida Driver License Bureau offices.

☐ **4.) Register Automobile(s).** Register your automobile(s) and obtain a Florida license plate at the tax collector's office in the Florida county where you reside.

☐ **5.) Apply for Homestead Exemption.** Apply for the Florida homestead exemption at the property appraiser's office in the Florida county where your home is located.